THE OPENING
OF THE WAY

THE OPENING
OF THE WAY

*A Practical Guide to the
Wisdom Teachings of
Ancient Egypt*

ISHA SCHWALLER de LUBICZ

Inner Traditions International
Rochester, Vermont

Inner Traditions International
One Park Street
Rochester, Vermont 05767

First published in French by Editions Aryana, Paris
Copyright © 1979 by Editions Aryana
Translation copyright © 1981 by Inner Traditions

Library of Congress Cataloging-in-Publication Data

Schwaller de Lubicz, Isha, 1885—
The opening of the way.

Translation: of L'ouverture du chemin.
Includes index.
1. Occult sciences. I. Title.
BF 1999.S361613   299'.31   81-782
ISBN 0-89281-572-8   AACR2

Printed and bound in the United States

10   9   8   7   6   5   4   3   2   1

Distributed to the book trade in Canada by Publishers Group West (PGW),
Toronto, Ontario

Distributed to the book trade in the United Kingdom by
Deep Books, London

Distributed to the book trade in Australia by Millennium Books,
Newtown, N.S.W.

Distributed to the book trade in New Zealand by
Tandem Press, Auckland

Distributed to the book trade in Europe by
HDG Distrirep, The Netherlands

Distributed to the book trade in South Africa by
Alternative Books, Randburg

Contents

Introduction   1

PART ONE
   1. Freedom of Individual Search   11
   2. The Great Question   13
   3. The Human Constitution   17
   4. Soul and Consciousness   29
   5. The Aim   39
   6. The Duel   43

PART TWO
   7. The Way of the Heart   55
   8. The Fountain   63
   9. Knowledge   65
  10. The Discernment of Discernment   75
  11. The Milieu   77
  12. The Visit to the Cave   85
  13. The Sexual Problem   91
  14. The Pendulum   95
  15. Watchfulness and Mediation   101
  16. Conduct   105

PART THREE
  17. The Seven Accomplishments   113
  18. The Seven Obstacles   127

PART FOUR
  19. Reincarnation and Karma   143
  20. The Masters   153
  21. The Elite   161

PART FIVE
  22. Second Visit to the Cave   167
  23. Peace   177
  24. Joy   181
  25. "Son of Man" and "Son of God"   183
  26. Signature   187

Appendix I:
The Functional Relationships of Bodily Organs   189
Appendix II:
Psychospiritual States in Different Traditions   199

Index   205

Introduction

Modern man is the product of several centuries of cerebral culture; he has taught himself so much that he imagines he can progress unaided, simply regarding evolution as the logical development and mutual adaptation of cells, organs, and faculties.

This state of mind professes to explain the universe and man by reason and reason only, without supposing there to be any creative cause. It has, of course, strenthened the notion of free will; for if man has no other cause to consider beyond himself, if he is supreme in nature and the rational faculty supreme in man, then obviously he cannot admit the existence of any natural laws or forces other than those which his reasoning faculty can analyze; and this faculty seems to him to exist as a logical means of subjecting natural forces to his control. Research into human nature has therefore taken a biological, chemical, and largely mechanistic direction, with a purely analytical and Cartesian view of science, and has come up with no constructive answers to the question of how life ought to be lived.

But science, oriented thus to the increase of material comfort, has created new needs, and these in turn have developed in man a keen sense of envy and a terrible sense of haste. The Envy has become a social malady, and the sense of haste is so tyrannical that much thought is spent on trying to satisfy the need for it. Hence the feverish search for anything which will indulge the senses and the emotions, until in the end an emotional stimulus is valued only for its violence; but whether the effect of its indulgence is good or harmful, nobody knows or cares.

The life of the senses, when indulged so far, becomes extremely exacting. It is simple enough to arouse one's physical appetites, but not so easy to control them. Nerves trained to excitement feel an unhealthy craving for it, and when the life of brain and senses has been accustomed to be fed continually from without by an unending flow of secondhand thoughts and images, of catchy tunes and twitching rhythms, it calls for these things because they render individual effort superfluous, and shake to pieces any notion of real values. That is our modern world, dancing the infernal roundelay of haste, ever more deeply involved in the quest for variety and novelty.

A mind trained to these frantic gymnastics will clearly show two characteristics: It will be insatiable, always preferring quantity to quality, and it will suffer from the need for speed.

The quantitative mentality has done much already to transform the social pattern, producing a loss of interest in quality; and the need for speed has been transforming the lives of all humanity by abolishing distance, bringing nations and races dangerously close together without giving them any principle of concord.

But the worst effect of all these new impulses has been the nervous imbalance which cannot tolerate silence or inactivity—these two pillars of meditation, without which one can have no true intuition or spiritual experience. It may be objected that many inspirations, inventions, and even spiritual conversions have happened suddenly, without any preceding meditation; but the objection is unfounded because, however sudden a flash of intuition, it can only be perceived by one in a receptive state, that is one capable of catching the moment of inspiration and allowing it to gestate in attentive silence.

It is not difficult to show that this condition of readiness—which is stillness of the nerves and brain and heart—is hardly compatible with an impatient appetite which in modern man is exaggerated into an imperious need of the nerves and senses. For a need demands satisfaction, and the effort to satisfy it has disoriented our moral sense and our whole consciousness.

On the deepest level, consciousness is the perception by our inner being of all the experiences that come to us. Physical consciousness can be involuntary, as when a burn produces in some part of the body a sudden awareness and shrinking from the fire; but our cerebral consciousness is always the servant of our various appetites. The most common illustration is when heart and head agree to oblige each other by both obeying the appetites; they find excuses for one another, and between them create a pattern of consciousness, whose secret origin one professes to be ignorant of.

This disorientation of consciousness has led us to the denial of three essential qualities:

First, we deny the constant intervention of the Creative Word, inasmuch as the modern mind discovers as much First Cause as it requires in the activity of our cells, their faculties, and their logical progress toward mutual adaptation.

Second, spiritual inspiration and animation are denied, inasmuch as the acceptance of this idea would reduce the scope of pure reason and deprive it of the virtue of being self-created.

Third, there is denial of the harmonious relationship of all parts of our universe; for the understanding of this is not to be reached by intellectual search alone, but only by the path of silence and true meditation.

Yet, thanks to our greater ease of contact with other cultures, we now have many records of the direct perception of abstract realities, or of psychic influence exerted on living beings and natural objects. Europeans, when they witness such phenomena among peoples whom they call barbaric or backward, are surprised to find that there exists a traditional metaphysical background that is handed down by initiation. And though the methods of applying this knowledge are different in every tribe and culture, the essential condition is everywhere the same: namely, the communion of the initiates with the great spiritual principle whose name alone is different depending on religion or doctrine.

The development of man's mental faculties is the characteristic task of the West, but it has been misdirected making a means into an end; and the intensive development of these faculties in the latest stage of our evolution has given us nowadays a distorted notion of the extent of our human powers. Rational information has usurped the throne of Knowledge, and has declared valueless the heritage of ancient wisdom, which might cause it to lose its throne.

The learned rationalist wants above all things to avoid encountering, where doubt and knowledge meet, the one power which could limit his own, a ''divine'' power which he could neither analyze nor check.

And our learned man is in some danger of meeting this ''divine'' power—the Spirit, as he might properly call it—within himself. For that which incarnated at his birth received the impression of a spiritual impulse, which has a universal significance, though colored by his individual nature. Had his understanding been aroused so as to develop this first spiritual impulse, he would have been able to prevent his analytical reasoning faculty from acting like an angel of death to prevent the birth of his ''divine'' self from the depths of the primal paradise.

That this is possible has been proved by the appearance at various crises in human history of a sage who, by not permitting his rational judgment to interfere, was able to remain in contact with the Creative Word he was to express, and thus reveal to the world some spark of the divine wisdom.

If they are disposed to receive it, this spark of truth does give a moment of inspiration to those it touches; but they must then go through the same experience as happens after birth: If the spark is received and brooded over by the immortal being incarnate in the body, then it causes him to grow and increase his power; but if it is only received by the faculty of rational judgment, then the intellect will seize upon it and alter it to its own advantage, according to its preconceptions. And this intellect, acting as usual like an angel of separation, arranges its arbitrary code of good and evil so as to further its own control.

This interference by the reasoning faculty results in sterility; total awareness can no longer develop. Like a piece of earth deprived of its natural fertilizers, the rationalist receives no other nourishment than the arguments handed out by his intellect; and the latter develops only slowly, being influenced by nothing but the painful stresses and accidents of normal life.

One might suppose that this consequence would have put men on their guard and induced them to seek a remedy. But not at all. Lucifer is an angel of light, and his appearance will always deceive the worldly. Moreover, the serpent which sowed discord between Adam and Eve is the very incarnation of that greed which creates in man the hunger for quantity and then, to satisfy that, the infernal thirst for activity.

And if anyone, be he Buddha, Christ, or sage, dares to denounce this error, he is at once suspected of an assault on the ''happiness'' of the human race—that is, on its freedom to perpetuate its slavery on earth.

TOWARD THE ONE TRUTH

Modern inventions have brought East and West closer together, and given us back some contact with the sages of old time. Many sacred texts have been translated into European languages. Their inner meaning, of course, has not been revealed, for that requires a perfect knowledge not only of the language and letters but also of the symbolism. Yet enough light has been shed from the ancient wisdom to arouse interest among modern people.

The architecture of Egypt and of the East bears witness to undeniable achievements in geometry, mathematics, and cosmogony. Of those civilizations, the most ancient and long-lived seems to have been the period of the pharaohs; for the most ancient Greek and Chinese cultures were followed by gieological cataclysms and floods, and have left no remains.

About 3000 B.C. the Pyramid Texts were already speaking with authority of the constitution of man, his survival of death, and his relation to the life of the cosmos. Much later, Moses, who ''was learned in all the wisdom of the Egyptians'' (Acts 7:22), included in the Pentateuch as much of it as was suitable for his people; and out of this tradition came Christianity.

The first 5 books of the old Testament GR: Tool-book

In the meanwhile Lao-tse had illuminated the path of pure wisdom with the essential precepts of the Tao, and the Buddha had given to his disciples the law and the example of nonviolence and compassion.

During these millennia the dynasties of pharaohs had developed in symbolic terms the evolution of the royal principle (that is, of superhumanity) in the individual. Of this the pharaoh himself was the prototype, first in his Osirian development, then in his further evolution as Horus. And this evolution was also related to astronomical periods.

Until the coming of the Christ, the Egyptian sages brought to perfection their teaching in written texts and on their monuments; and ultimately they recapitulated in the Ptolemaic temple of Philae the whole symbolism of Isis and Osiris in relation to man and Nature, and also that of Horus, which had hitherto been reserved for the initiates of the temple and now became the very foundation of the mission of Christ.

After this the initiations of the Essenes were the link between the wisdom of Egypt, the metaphysic of St. John, the pure mysticism of the first three centuries of the Christian Church in Asia Minor, Africa, and Europe, and finally the philosophical symbolism of the Byzantines.

In the fourth century began the assertion of the temporal power of the church, and its political activity, with the interminable disputes of theologians and synods. The schism of 1054 between Byzantium and Rome did not prevent the Crusaders from bringing back to Europe the knowledge of Byzantine symbolism, which is the basis of that of our great cathedrals. Thus, in spite of theological differences, the Coptic and Abyssinian churches, who were the first Christians in Africa, as well as the Orthodox and Roman churches, were all united by the symbolism they had received from Egypt, and which had been handed down in sculpture and architecture, in liturgy and ritual.

This unity of tradition, showing them all to be founded on the same original understanding, was the best evidence of their essential soundness. It is regrettable that a strict dictatorship, inspired by the wish for temporal power, should have used the threat of excommunication to put practical and sometimes even indefensible commandments on the same footing as indisputable dogmas. The consequences were the Lutheran and Calvinist schisms; and the violent reaction of Catholicism, for all its bloodshed, neither prevented the success of Protestantism nor corrected its own abuses. The cause of Catholicism was more hindered than helped both by the martyrdom of the templar sages, and by the torture inflicted by the Inquisition on men who practiced an individual quest for knowledge.

Yet this does not entitle us to attack the Christian message, which came to the world at the date required by cosmic harmony, and gave humanity proof that union is possible between the divine and the human. For all the great traditions have spoken of man on earth as in a transitory condition between his original state of nonseparation and his final conscious return to union with the divine.

The trouble came from man's desire to possess, wield, and know by means of his brain and senses, all the powers that he knew in himself before being separated from it. This is why the Gospel declares that to enter the kingdom of heaven one must become as a little child; that is, must let the mind obey the impulses which come from the heart and spirit.

All the great messengers of the Spirit, and the masters of mysticism, have declared with one voice that the supreme aim of humanity is reunion with its divine principle. As means to this end they all mention simplicity of heart and mind and the abolition of hatred, violence, and vengeance, even when these are given the pretext of rectifying the human conscience. These teachers have never been guilty of theological quarreling or theocratic dictatorship, nor can their teaching be impugned by those who have. But to attack the latter and expose the reasons for their fanaticism would only be another mistake and would give rise to futile acrimony.

Attack implies a wish to be right and to overcome an adversary. Where worldly expediency is the object it can be effective, but in the spread of the enlightenment of the human consciousness it can only hinder, because its arbitrary interference prevents errors from proving themselves to be so.

Lao-tse defines wisdom as "complete willingness to be the plaything of chance circumstances." This, says he, is why the sage is able to accomplish the great designs of nonactivity. And these "great designs of nonactivity" are the will of our Father in heaven, whose will must be done on earth as in heaven. The teaching is the same in both cases, and both teachers insist on simplicity of heart and mind. "Unless ye become as little children, ye shall not enter the kingdom of heaven," said the Christ. Lao-tse said: "The mind of the man of established virtue may be compared to that of a newborn child. He does not seem to suspect that poisonous insects bite or sting, that the claws of wild beasts can rend and the talons of birds of prey can tear. . . . Such men can express luminous truths in the most ordinary language."

The Buddha likewise preached the abolition of hatred and discord, and rejected complexity of doctrine. He made true understanding consist in the direct vision of that which cannot be put in writing, and in the communion of the spirit.

The Christ said: "Woe unto you, lawyers, for ye have taken away the key of knowledge: ye entered not in yourselves, and them that were entering in ye hindered" (Luke 11:52). And although Jesus was born of Israel, and came to fulfill the Law and the Prophets, it was to a Samaritan woman, and enemy of the Jews, that he taught the only true way of worship: "Woman, believe me, the hour cometh, when ye shall neither in this mountain, nor yet at Jerusalem, worship the Father" (John

4:21). "But the hour cometh, and now is, when the true worshippers shall worship the Father in spirit and in truth: for the Father seeketh such to worship him. God is Spirit; and they that worship him must worship him in spirit and in truth" (John 4:23-24).

This saying no other wisdom can contradict, because, being universal, it brings peace to all those who are seeking in spirit and in truth. Every sincere seeker has in his heart this "will toward the light," and if he listens to it he will not seek in vain. For he will know that behind all religions there is only one Truth, and the revelation of this truth through their different myths and symbols brings harmony instead of discord. This clarification will only be resisted by those who want to obscure the original teaching in order to assure their own control over the minds and consciences of men.

The difficulty of the present age is caused by the confused variety of beliefs and opinions. The restlessness of our daily life, and the falsity of conventional artificial standards in morality and aesthetics, have corrupted our vision, until it seems that nothing short of catastrophe can arouse us to a truer awareness. We confuse the discernment of reality with our personal opinion, and intellectual judgment with recognition of truth.

The recognition of truth means discerning true form false and pure from impure, and must always be related to our aim in making such a distinction. Should our aim be to reject the impure altogether, or to discern how much of it can be transmuted into the pure? If the latter, whoever is to decide must have in his nature something of the impure as well as the pure.

To take an example, the lead which is used for purifying gold is carried off with the impurities, while the gold remains; and so the utilitarian mind would say that in this operation the gold is the true judge of purity. The wisdom of the Egyptians, however, thought otherwise; for the name of "judge" was given to the imperfect thing which avails to separate pure and impure.

This imperfect thing is human nature, and the physical body is the vehicle of the consciousness built up by the experiences of life. But if this consciousness is to mediate and discern effectively, it must be free to undergo its experiences uncorrupted by artifical notions and conventional rules. Otherwise the imperfect thing will reject the pure instead of being transmuted by it.

The "pure" is the immortal element in man, his divine soul or, in Egyptian terms, his higher *Ka*;* it is the Christlike or Horuslike element which, by its union with the corporeal man, makes the latter a complete

*See Appendix II.

consciousness and teaches him to distinguish real values from relative values.

This notion fills our mortal personality with dread, and it fights to the last ditch. That is why the cornerstone—the Christ manifested—will always be a stumbling block to the human intellect; for Reality must always appear as a judgment upon the error which refuses to acknowledge it.

Because our values have been corrupted, our mortal world is enveloped in a gathering storm. There must obviously occur in life on earth crises from time to time, when all those elements of human nature which can possibly seem to possess free will burst like prisoners from a jail and all violently attack one another with mutual hatred, each blaming the other for the tumult which none of them understand. At such a time the voice of a sage will not be heard; the fury must first abate.

But if after the tempest we hope for calm to be restored, we must acknowledge that serenity can only be established by wisdom founded upon true understanding. And this wisdom has never been denied to humanity, although it has only been made manifest at the appropriate time and place.

Spirit, being universal, has never revealed itself through one exclusive interpreter. All races and all epochs have produced their great ones who have shown what wisdom and power can be attained by the man who knows how to cultivate in himself those sacred gifts. Yet just as a crystal cannot form except in a solution of its proper nature, but will then form other similar crystals around itself, so the world cannot be enlightened by the incarnation of a single elect spirit; for this world will not be transformed unless there are present other elements able to receive the message and bring it to fruition.

These elements will never be more than a minority, an elite group. Consciousness, in the mass of humanity, is still too vague for the experience of an individual spiritual calling, and these elements will therefore always remain in flocks and herds, prudently on the lookout.

But any man who does not wish to be carried away by the tempestuous instability of the mass should have the courage nowadays to seek the light for himself, freely and without restraint. For today is a new phase of development, and there is already a gulf between yesterday and today.

The disturbances of our chaotic age have at least had the advantage that they have overthrown the barriers and shaken the values which society dared to alter. Instead of waiting for this old construction to collapse upon our heads, we should be wise to dig down quickly and find the indestructible foundations of the ancient wisdom. The aim of this work is to aid in this rediscovery.

PART ONE

1

Freedom of Individual Search

Have we the right to claim the freedom of individual search?

It would be unwise to give too absolute an answer, for the answer must depend on the stage of evolution of the individual's consciousness, on his convictions, and often on his courage. One should never try to force understanding on those who cannot or will not listen.

Equally, the flesh of a fruit must be distinguished from its kernel, and the mass of humanity from the elite who can become its growing point. The latter are the "chosen" in that they are prepared to develop themselves to the suprahuman state; they are "called" to the reconstruction of the conscious Cosmic Man, each one being a cell of his body [a "Number-entity"].

Among the chosen there are two categories. First are those who are no longer entirely satisfied by the explanations of Western dogma, and yet are still deeply attached to certain religious observances. These should never be urged to abandon the practice of their cult, for ritual and communal prayer are a strong moral support, and without them the "liberated" man is in some danger of confusing freedom of experience with *mere absence of morality*.

Second, there are those who feel an imperious need to seek the Light outside of dogmatic prohibitions and ritual obligations. These should be told the truth that Buddhist mystics teach their disciples: Hitherto you needed ritual, cults, and images to comfort you in your earthly life, to channel your passions and direct your mind toward a higher world. But if you wish to find deliverance and create in yourself the conditions of eternal life, you should give up doctrinal obligations whenever they interfere with the freedom of your quest.

The Christ also had an answer for such seekers, when He said that God must be worshipped "in spirit and in Truth." However, we need to know what is meant by "in spirit and in truth."

Buddhism teaches very rightly that ignorance is an obstacle to deliverance, and ignorance includes wrong beliefs which prevent individual experience by means of rigid doctrines or intellectual and moral restrictions.

Nothing encourages selfish amorality more than the excuse of blind belief and the certainty of pardon, especially when one need not even sincerely fulfill the conditions for obtaining the pardon.

The ideas of fault, sin, condemnation, and pardon have only a very relative value unless we look at the reality behind them. Faults committed against an established convention are a matter for the community or the social order; but as regards "real" sins, what man can judge the sins of another, not being able to read his conscience and see his real motives?

The evil which makes a man a sinner in reality resides not in the act itself, but in offending against one's own conviction. And this remains true, whether or not the conviction is justified. For the conviction, unless it be an artificial intellectual construction, is the product of the *present* consciousness of the individual, and in obeying it he is obeying what is truth for him *at present;* and even if the result is unfortunate, he will remain essentially innocent, though he had to abide the temporal consequences. In other words, the experience will enlarge his consciousness without retarding its final unification. If, on the other hand, his conviction is based on rational arguments, the unfortunate consequences of error can enlighten his consciousness if he understands them; if not, a dimming of consciousness will result until he learns how to eliminate rationalizations from his judgments.

The lack of convictions—that is, of vigilant consciousness—is a state not of innocence, but a state of stupidity in which a man loses both his sense of responsibility and his feeling for human experience.

Equally, blind submission to denominational authority is an excuse for killing the sense of responsibility, and prevents the growth of discernment.

For one only learns by what one suffers in one's own person and experiences within oneself. And the only help that can be given is advice regarding the correctness of the aim and the efficacy of the means.

No one can be transformed by the experience of another. He who would realize his suprahuman Unity must leave the herd and set out along to explore his own self, and, through himself, the universe.

2

The Great Question

There are moments when, for all the distractions of daily life, one comes to a standstill, and with a dazed feeling of panic or discouragement, puts to oneself the fatal question: "What's the use?"

For the present let us stop and listen in silence to the anguish of this question. The silence that it evokes is terrible, like the silence of night, with a clock marking the end of yet another hour. It is a question as cold as a marble tomb, and gives one a shiver of loneliness. For who can answer it?

We all know that, to escape this moment of panic, we accept any answer that may be offered; and there are plenty of people willing to offer one. To the crowd, to normal people, silence is intolerable; something must be said, no matter what, to fill the void, and conceal this warning of the existence of something infinite and other.

This attitude distinguishes West from East more clearly than any frontier. The Westerner, to soothe his anxiety, explores the realm of thought, reads books, compares opinions, questions other thinkers, and in fact looks for the answer outside himself. The Oriental, more contemplative, begins by closing his own circuit; he crosses hands and feet, and then in the little world within he listens to the resonance of the greater world without, in a contemplation which is more dreaming than thinking. And this is no mere literary metaphor; it is like the waking dream of a wild animal which, as it lies relaxed, picks up the very slightest pulsations and reactions of the life around it.

The aim is to hear within oneself the appeals, the regrets, and the warnings which are normally stifled by the activity of daily life; and to explore and clarify with courage one's secret awareness of certainties and uncertainties, desires and dissatisfaction, which in the normal routine of life we fail to formulate clearly because of habit, shame, or fear of what others will think. And yet the opinions of others are the worst excuse that we can have. For they, as they drag us along in the daily round, are simply reacting, according to their personal pattern, to the cares of the moment. In facing the drama of his own soul a man is always alone.

Indeed this great question does involve us in a real drama. Life is only a dismal farce if the end of all our incoherent struggles is nothing but the grave. But if there is a sensible answer, if life on earth has a motive and a purpose higher than that of mere banal existence, then this motive and purpose have surely been discernible through the ages of human history.

Why then has this question excited so much hatred and bloodshed, so many absurd controversies? Peasants do not quarrel about the proper season to reap or sow; the need to eat has made them obedient to the laws of nature. Man could find a similar law, a law of cosmic seasons and human epochs, if he would study the laws of his own becoming, and their expression in the successive traditions of different races.

Who would maintain that the season of harvest is wiser than that of sowing, or condemn the dormancy of the seed in winter as a deplorable waste of time? But no less absurd are our disputes about the means employed by heaven or by the sages to awaken the conscience of humanity, when we try to judge by our present notions of understanding the teaching suitable to another day.

If we want to find the answer to our anxiety, we must first clarify it by trying to distinguish the real in it from the merely relative. And this means that we must cease to compare and condemn the points of view of ages which had a mental background different from our own. We must first leap outside all doctrines whatsoever and frankly put to ourselves the two questions which directly interest us: "What is the value and aim of human life?" "Is there a Power whose will has fixed this aim and the means of its attainment?" If so, why does it leave us in ignorance of the aim, manipulating us like puppets? But if not, man is simply the plaything of natural forces and of the egotism of others, obliged, like them, to protect his own self.

And in either case, why do we sometimes revolt against this self, which can never be satisfied with aspiration to a grade above its own? Can this self be in revolt against itself? If not, then what in oneself is opposing it?

Can the answer to these questions be discovered within ourselves, or must we look for it outside? If we look for it in some teaching or other, what criterion shall we use to judge the value of the teaching? If our own conscience is to judge, what is this conscience to which we apply for a decision?

In most men what they call conscience is a record of ideas, impressions, and convictions put together by deliberate thought and education; but the awareness thus formed is as fleeting as the reflection of clouds in a mirror. Nor is it really our own, since it can be modified by various influences. Nothing of this composite effect will survive the dissolution of our physical body with its emotional and mental constituents. This is a cerebral consciousness, not a part of our immortal being.

But how many men on earth have consciously awakened their real conscience, which would make them truly knowing and responsible? In order to speak ''consciously,'' we must first agree on words, then investigate the means to awaken this conscience.

SELF-KNOWLEDGE

To avoid confusion, let us agree about the meaning of such words as ''soul,'' ''consciousness,'' ''self-knowledge,'' the multifarious interpretations of which bring about disputes as fruitless as those of the Tower of Babel. And unless we are to make of the human being nothing but an intelligent animal which decays in the grave, our study of the human constitution will have to include a consideration of its immortal elements, by whatever name they are to be called.

And just as modern science admits that energy can exist in different states, some more degraded than others, so too should man try to recognize in himself those states of subtle energy which are his immortal element.

If he knows nothing of them, he lowers himself to the condition of an intelligent animal, and attributes to his brain phenomena which really depend on his higher faculties.

But if he learns to recognize them, he becomes aware of his immortal self, and attains the privileges of a realm superior to that of the animal man. In this work the animal man, with the intellectual faculties dependent on his mortal brain, is called the Automaton, or Automatic Self. In order to keep it functioning harmoniously, the first requisite is a knowledge of the laws which govern it.

The more subtle states of man are studied in Chapter 4, ''Levels of Consciousness,'' and their correspondences with the major spiritual traditions are given in Appendix II under the heading ''Psychospiritual States.''

3
The Human Constitution

THE TWO WILLS

That a human being can aspire to a higher state shows him to be dissatisfied with his present state; and such dissatisfaction reveals, latent within him, a form of consciousness other than mere animal consciousness.

But whether a man ignores this opportunity to progress or tries to follow it up, and whether or not he succeeds, it does demonstrate the existence of two divergent wills, corresponding to two different levels of being. One level is that of the animal man, which I shall call the Automaton because it depends on the interplay of its physical, mental, and emotional constituents. The other, to be described in Chapter 4, shows a higher and more subtle awareness than that of the Automaton. The two wills may be called the Personal Will and the Will to the Light.

When the Will to the Light begins to make itself felt, there follows inevitably a struggle with the Personal Will, because the two have different objectives and, even more important, do not understand one another. Harmony can only be established if they can be brought to agree, and this requires self-knowledge.

The Automaton is the foundation of our higher states of being, so its constitution should be the first object of study and observation.

Psychology and physiology, as classically taught, have unfortunately complicated themselves with a multiplicity of theories and a detailed analysis of every constituent element and every aspect of every function, when in fact only a synthetic view can reveal the laws of their development and of their vital interplay.

In another direction, many students have tried to enlarge their knowledge of the human constitution by observing its correspondences with the planets and the elements. Of course, as an inhabitant of the planet Earth, man has in himself all the correspondences of the solar system in which this planet moves; and the planetary correspondences of every part of the body have been defined in astrology. These relationships are interesting because therapeutic treatment can be based on the analogies between planets, plants, and metals, always provided that the practitioner has a thorough knowledge of all the vital functions and how they may affect the different states of consciousness. For this reason this very complicated study has an esoteric side which cannot safely be made public.

The knowledge of cosmic law on which this knowledge was based is part of a tradition of wisdom that was only taught in genuine centers of initiation. Without this knowledge the occult sciences will be dangerously subjective, with only a vague reflection of the authentic tradition.

Fortunately their study is not indispensable to the attainment of full consciousness. For this full realization is the "one thing necessary," and to this all else will be added. The most dangerous obstacles to it are curiosity after knowledge (for it disperses attention), complexity of systems and opinions, and the method of analysis by dissociation.

There is, of course, a great temptation to interpret "self-knowledge" as an analytical observation of one's psychic reactions, separating out the physical, emotional, and mental sources of feeling in order to control their origins and interdependence. Strict training can effect this result, but its finest fruit (already very hard to attain) can only be full control of the Automatic Self, that is, of the whole physical, emotional, and mental life. Such control can give one certain psychic powers over oneself and others, but only influences the lower human levels; for the method of dissociation is hostile to any contact with the spiritual nature, whose method is synthesis and union. In such a case the voice of the Spiritual self, on the rare occasions when it can make itself heard, will arouse nothing but vague disquiet, an anxiety caused by the impossibility of establishing contact between two states of being so totally dissimilar.

Dissection, or even vivisection, can show the physical constitution of an organism, but will never reveal the secret workings of those vital energies whose normal course it has altered or even interrupted. It will never reveal the magnetic power by which each organ draws its particular nourishment from the arterial blood, which provides the same irrigation for all the body. How then can we explain the mysterious affinity which causes different types of cells to specialize the blood into its own nature? The transmutation and assimilation of the same matter into the different energies proper to each organ will remain a secret to the anatomist, just as the transmutation of vital sexual or nervous energy into spiritual forces can never be understood by any method based on either dissociation or willpower.

If we wish to acquire the "one thing necessary" in our knowledge of the human constitution, we must study it in such a way as to reveal the interdependence of its different elements, and show how they can be consciously controlled.

In studying the human Automaton from the point of view of synthesis, we must consider first the relation of the various organs to the bloodstream and to the sources of vital energy; then correctly attribute them to the functional groups in which they belong; and finally also group them in their regions of mutual influence, without which no true diagnosis is possible

This study, being too technical to stand in the text, has been given in Appendix I. The object here is to present a simple but comprehensive view of the unity of the human constitution and the interplay of its vital functions. With this knowledge we shall become aware of the harmony which governs them and relates them to the corresponding functions in the universe. We shall also learn how to keep them in equilibrium by acting upon one through the medium of others.

Diseases are frequently made worse by a dissociative treatment which attacks the morbid consequences and does not touch the cause. Man is a universe in which the higher conditions can influence the lower if only they are allowed to do so. But in medicine as in psychology, organic disorders should be cured by setting right the "milieu"; local action should be no more than provisional.

We shall study as we proceed the means of putting man's various milieus into favorable conditions; but first let us accept into our intellectual milieu the few essential notions that will direct our thought according to our synthetical point of view.

CONSTITUTION OF THE AUTOMATON

Man's physical being is composed of five bodies, four of which are materially perceptible; the fifth can only be recognized by the sensitiveness of its points of contact. The five are:

1. A bony body, the skeleton
2. A body of flesh, consisting of the envelopes of skin, and the muscular, fibrous, and connective tissues
3. A body of vessels or reservoirs, with rivers, streams, and reservoirs
4. A body of generating stations and channels for the nervous force, namely the nervous system with the spinal marrow, encephalon, and nerves
5. A body of "lines of force" or "meridians, exteriorized in the skin as

sensitive points which reveal by reflexes the state of the organs to which they severally correspond.

These five bodies are so harmoniously associated that they are mutually dependent, each having its own nature, rhythm, and role. Together they constitute a complete universe of operating stations, which work together to create, maintain, and transform the substances required for the existence of the animal body.

The more subtle states of being, which give man his advantage over the animals, have their physical points of contact in certain vital centers through which the Automaton is able to open up a connection with them.

Our individual world, made in the image of the greater world, has its sun and planets, its cardinal points and poles, its hell and paradise and limbo. If a man really learned to know himself, he could discover which of these his present attitude would lead him to occupy on the other side of death.

The most tangible manifestation of the World of Causes is in the functions which regulate our existence. These functions are incarnated in our bodies in the form of organs which are specific forms of consciousness. We may call them organs or planets, speak of the heart or of the sun; in either case we are only referring to a particular functional manifestation of the one life.

Our solar system has an active center, the sun, whose globe is the visible body animated by the true invisible sun, the center of all its power. So too the heart is the central vessel of exchange which regulates the flow of the blood and carries animate life. But the animating fire, seat of the spiritual life and source of the ''Intelligence of the Heart,'' is the occult or spiritual heart. Focused between the physical heart and the solar plexus, the whole cardiac area is its radiating sphere.

The activity of the planets is analogous to that of the bodily organs, and all the stations of the celestial zodiac have their living representatives in the metabolic stations of energy in the body.

There are thus three manifestations of the energy which animates us: the nervous system, anatomically recognized; the exterior longitudinal system of ''meridians''; and the circuit of zodiacal centers of the ''secret fire,'' vitalized by the triple serpent of fire in the spinal column.

It is important to understand how the entire organism cooperates in maintaining this fire, whose inexhaustible source is cosmic Spirit. The lungs breathe it in with the air which purifies and animates the blood; the digestive organs, vitalized by the blood, transform it into animal heat by the dissolution and transmutation of foodstuffs; and the final product of digestion, the sublimated chyle, brings to the blood and thence to the spinal marrow the specific energies created by the processes of assimilation. Then the secret fire in the spinal column performs the last transmutation, in which the ultimate fire of human genesis is reunited to the Fire of its origin.

The only thing still needed in this work is one final link, and this depends not upon animal automatism but on the spiritual decision of the individual. This link is the ultimate ensoulment by that longing which can draw directly on the Divine Source of all things; and, by this miracle of Love, "Myself" exteriorizes into "the Self" and attains the fusion which breaks the closed circle of its egocentricity.

We should try to feel the living synthesis of all these manifold concentrating circuits which combine their functions in unceasing cooperation. For the same generative processes repeat themselves unceasingly at all stages of the transformations of being, both in the universe and in ourselves. We can study them separately, and try to experience them severally, only if we remember that, despite the succession of phases in any given transformation, nevertheless the many different stages of the vital process work simultaneously and cannot properly be separated.

The next synthetical aspect to be considered is its orientation of the body comparable to that of the earth.

The body has an axis, the spine, and two poles: the south, which issues, and the north, which receives. These two poles are the sites of the two procreative worlds: at the south the sexual procreator, and at the north the mental procreator. Inside the body the two poles are indicated by two complementary glands: in the north the thyroid, belonging to the white principle, and in the south the adrenals, belonging to the black principle. These regulate the action and equilibrium of the three principles of Sulfur, Mercury, and Salt, and are the link between the body and the two procreators. Furthermore the thyroid, as north pole of the glandular system of the trunk, acts as intermediary between the adrenals and the pituitary gland in the brain.

The right side and hand are active and "give," while the left side and hand are passive and "receive."

The back is passive and sensitive, as are the posterior nerves of the spinal marrow.

All the organs which work together in the absorption, transformation, and assimilation of the matter required for physical life are situated in the anterior portion of the body.

The four limbs are living symbols of dualization, the legs for movement, the arms and hands for action.

The head is in itself an epitome of man, since all the functions of our organism, both apparent and occult, have their signal stations, or command posts, in the milieu of the brain. One could say that if the body is the world of types, specified as each organ and its component parts, the head is a likeness of the world of archetypes, the principles of "Becoming."

The front and back of the head are as different as the front and back of the body, for the nape of the neck continues energetic activity of the vertebral column, with essential vital points in the cervical vertebrae, the medulla oblongata, and the cerebellum. It is the summit of the Pillar of Osiris.

The face is the mirror of Horus (the Word or Logos), with the organs of the five senses, which are the five modes of expression of the Word. In it stand the two luminaries, the solar right eye and the lunar left eye, two globes whose eyelids create day and night; and the iris is a little zodiac in whose divisions is inscribed the state of all the organs in the body.

In the fetus, the two luminaries (the eyes) appear first; then the planets (the organs) begin to show one after another.

THE HUMORS

Four rivers watered the garden of Eden, and in the midst was hidden the Tree of Knowledge of Good and Evil.

The garden of our body is watered similarly by four humors. Two are perfect in their origin, and their colors are those of the two perfections of Nature: One is white, the lymph, lunar in character, the element that gives substance. The other is red, the blood, solar in character, the element that animates and vitalizes. These are the first elements of transsubstantiation.

The other two humors are imperfect because they are elements of fixation and separation: One is green, the bile, the element of separation and dissolution. The other is black, the atrabile, the element of contraction.

These four humors are in two couples, like two rivers each of two streams, having different qualities but the same origin.

Not without reason did the ancients call them "humors," for according to their predominance in man's organism they color and influence the character of the individual.

The bile is corrosive and tends to aggressivity and bitterness; the atrabile is astringent and tends to melancholy, anxiety, and doubt. These two serve the egoistic will.

The blood and lymph are more altruistic. The red blood is a powerful regenerator, and its humor is confident and generous. It is the vehicle of the lower "sensitive soul," which corresponds to the Hebrew *nefesh* and the animal *Ba* of the Egyptians, the animal vital force or "animal soul," whose departure means the death of the body.

The white lymph is the body's nurse. At the slightest danger it sacrifices its leukocytes, which rush to the threatened point and use themselves up in building a barrage against infection.

These are the transmitters of animate life.

The working of the four humors both can and should be held in balance, for any disorder will result in useless conflict.

SYNTHESIS AND COORDINATION OF THE VITAL FORCES

The table of functional groups (see Appendix I) shows what organs cooperate in creative action on the physical plane. The mutual relationships and dependence of the various organs invite us to study the possibility of controlling them and of working out a therapy which would keep them in balance.

The most important thing to observe and understand is the physical and psychic relationship of the organs, especially as they influence our different psychic and spiritual states; also, of course, their relationship to the two procreative worlds, the cerebral and the sexual.

The liver and the spleen form a balance of psychic forces, as can be seen from their specific modes of reaction.

The liver contains the characteristics of the physical personality and its heredity, and these color the characteristics of sexual energy, of which it is the reservoir.

Although belonging to the central solar system of the heart, the liver, like Jupiter, acts as a personal sun; and like the sun in the zodiac, it has twelve functions (manufacture of blood and glucose, destruction of toxins, purification of the blood, and so forth).

Like Jupiter, the father of Mars, it generates the Martian bile. It rules its little exterior universe, consisting of brain and sex. Any ill-timed activity of the bile immediately stimulates the brain activity and sets up a chain reaction of associations of ideas, leading to irritation and feelings of personal willfulness, and so rapid is the circuit that it gives the impression of being simultaneous (bile—brain—liver—spleen—bile, etc.).

Jupiter is called in Egypt "the star of the south," which is perfectly correct, for Jupiter-Amon-Min is the procreative energy; the liver is the energetic sun of the sexual world and the ego. In it resides the "seed" of the permanent Personal Consciousness, which, if awakened, can keep it in equilibrium.

The liver is the autocrat of the body, and can be an agent of peace or wrath, according to how it obeys the suggestions of the central sun, the heart, or those of the three agents of the personal will, which are thinking will, sexual passion, and the egoism of the innate "I."

The Spleen

Unlike the liver, the spleen is in direct contact with the central sun of the organism, the physical and spiritual heart. In relation to the physical heart its role is earthy and Saturnian, transforming and harmonizing the white and red corpuscles and keeping them in balance. It has a peculiar connection with the pancreas, and these two, with the stomach, have an influence of proximity on the heart.

Psychically, as seat of the etheric (astral) form which carries the maternal heredity, it is in touch with the astral world or state, that is, the Akasha, in which is recorded the imaginative idea of everything which happens in our universe. It is thus, as the Chinese teach, the seat of the imaginative power, and reacts physically to personal emotions.

It is also, with the spiritual heart, the region which reacts to the Spiritual Consciousness, and thus can be the occult seat of conscious discernment, and of the individual conscience or *Maat,* being in contact both with this reality and with the powers of imagination and emotion.

If emotion and the Saturnian function prevail against the suggestions of the Spiritual Consciousness, the resulting discord produces splenetic behavior, just as discord in the functions of the liver produces anger or tears.

The Heart

The nature and function of the heart cannot be understood apart from the cardiac region which provides its driving force. The sun that vitalizes the physical heart is the spiritual heart, which is a center of spiritual fire which can be stirred up and strengthened by close attention and meditation.

The spiritual heart is the seat of the Presence, the magnet of our divine *Ka,* and its expression is that impersonal love which alone can prevail against all the fires of passion. It forms, together with the spleen, the area which reacts to the Spiritual Consciousness. By loving concentration it can become a radiant center of indestructible life.

The physical heart is its servant, the ''minister of the lord and master,'' as the Chinese sages call it. Its activator is ''the master of the heart.'' This is a functional command post, and it has its meridian of energy and its discoverable sensitive points just as if it were an organ.

The ''master of the heart'' is the agent for transmitting energy between the spiritual heart and the physical heart, and as such it is in relation both with the conscious mind and with the Automaton. It rules the heartbeat and the energy of the whole sexual region, which includes not only the sexual glands and organs but also, in this context, the kidneys.

The Chinese likewise call it ''the mother of the blood,'' because it regulates the flow of the blood, in conjunction with the small intestine, which refreshes and nourishes the blood with its chyle.

Thanks to this activator, the physical heart is the center and governor of the whole organism. For although the lungs are activated by the air and fire that they breathe in, the heart is the center and motor of the circuit which regenerates the blood in them.

Together with its region (the stomach, spleen, and pancreas)* the heart is the agent of combustion of the terrestrial food which is to become assimilable nourishment. It collects the blood, which carries the liquids provided by the kidneys and liver, and also the nourishing chyle distilled in the small intestine. But both the small intestine and the kidneys are regulated in their energic aspect by the "master of the heart."

This mutual dependence makes it understandable that the functioning of the organs can be improved through the intermediary of the heart; and conversely, the state of the heart depends on the balance of the organs serving it.

CONTROL OF THE CIRCUITS

Over and above the interdependence of the organs according to their relationship in type of energy, in proximity, and in function, we have to consider the circuits.

All distribution of liquids is performed by circuits whose equilibrium depends upon the heart. Thus are distributed energy, blood, and the products of digestion.

These circuits are controlled by the Three Heaters (respiratory, digestive, and sexual), which in turn are governed by the master of the heart.

Ultimately, therefore, everything depends on the master of the heart. And since the latter is the intermediary between the heart and the higher consciousness, through it the higher consciousness can act. Further, since the circuit which regenerates the blood (heart—lungs—heart) is under the control of the master of the heart, one can deliberately influence one's respiration either to calm oneself or to stimulate intense activity.

The circuit "master of the heart—kidneys—sex" makes it possible to transmute sexual force by the conscious action of the master of the heart. Equally, the circuit "liver—bile—brain" can be controlled by the Personal Consciousness,* which can observe the personal reactions of the Automaton and prevent them by cutting off the circuit between the bile and brain.

*See Appendix I.
*See Chapter 4.

These short examples are given in order to show the possibility of controlling the impulsive reactions of the Automatic Self by means of an awakened consciousness.

THE SOURCES OF ENERGY AND ANIMAL HEAT

A knowledge of functional relationships in the body does not actually explain the activity of the organs, for that depends upon an imponderable power visible only in its effects, which vary according to the degrees of its subtlety. It is usually called ''energy,'' meaning the source of all the essential phenomena of heat, movement, and vital stimulation, without which the organic functions could not perform their work.

Classical physiology recognizes it as the force conducted along the well-known routes of the nervous system, by which the body is made capable of movement and sensation.

The principal organic sources of animal heat are three: the lungs, the stomach with the large intestine, and the liver. The lungs serve to raise or lower the internal temperature and the speed of heartbeat. The stomach and large intestine produce animal heat and energy from the digestion of food. One of the twelve functions of the liver is to energize the blood, and sexual force depends upon its proper functioning.

The small intestine, on the other hand, is called in Egypt ''he who refreshes his brothers,'' because it cools the blood by feeding it with the lunar chyle, which is of a cold nature. For this reason inflammation here can be dangerous to the heart if it deprives the blood of this refreshing element by changing the cold nature of the chyle.

The ''energetic tree of life'' in the spine works with the nervous energy just as the ''distributive tree of life'' works with the circulation of the blood—added to which there are the plexuses of the sympathetic system and the even more subtle energies which run along the vertebral column and are called in Sanskrit *Ida, Pingala,* and *Shushumna.*

The most mysterious of the vital circuits is one hitherto unrecognized in the West, although it provides a key to the equilibrium of the bodily functions. The energy from this source flows imperceptibly along the ''meridians of acupuncture''* known in Chinese medicine; it stimulates the activity of the organs and at the same time draws energy from them. The energy flowing along these lines of force is derived from what the Chinese call the ''three heating powers,'' by which it affects respectively the respiratory, digestive, and sexual functions.

---

*See G. Soulié de Morand, *Acupuncture chinoise* (Paris: Mercure de France, 1939). [Appendix A.]

Finally, in order to understand the occult function of the heart, one must also remember the fourth source of energy, the master of the heart, which, together with the spiritual heart, constitutes the cardiac region, of which the physical heart is the visible manifestation.

THE FIRE OF LIFE

Thus by studying the organic functions we are led to consider their motive force, which is the Fire of Life that vitalizes them in their different ways and is in fact the essential agent of all the vital functions. For although the manifestations are many, there is only one source of all of them, namely the vital Fire which animates the world, the essential Light and causal principle of all that exists, called by the Evangelist John "the Word," and by the ancient Egyptians "Horus" (or, in its universal connotation, Horus the Elder, *Hor-wer*). In its human incarnation it was called the Christ by the Evangelists, and by the Egyptians "Horus of Men," or "the Horus who rises out of the limbs of the body." The Principle is one, though the name differs in every language; it remains the Spirit, the Light shining in darkness, the "Fire" of all the sages.

Fire, in its various aspects of heat, light, and destruction, is its manifestation. Imprisoned in matter, it is called the Dragon in China, and Ptah in Egypt. When dualized by its fall into Nature, its concretizing aspect is called Satanic, or Sethian in Egypt, and its liberating aspect is called Luciferic, or Horian. It produces all the aspects of energy, and the reactive aspect which it arouses in everything that exists is called life.

In the human body it shows itself as life in the organs and blood, and as energy in the spinal marrow and nervous system. On a more subtle plane it is *Ida* and *Pingala*, the double current of life flowing on the right and left sides of the curved wall of the spine and which, if it functions correctly, stimulates the spiritual current of the *Shushumna* to rise from the center of the marrow. This triple current is the "serpent-fire" of yoga, and it leads to the "coronal center," which is subtle and not physical. It is symbolized by the well-known diadem of Tutankhamon, in which a golden serpent comes up from the back of the neck over to the forehead, where it stands up out of a convolution representing the center of force.

The two currents of vital Fire, *Ida* and *Pingala*, were called in Egypt the "soul of Ra" and "soul of Osiris." The uraeus on pharaoh's brow (from *iâr*, that which rises) represents the vital Fire rising up to the frontal center on the forehead.

This Fire is the one source of energy, and its two aspects are called in China *yin* and *yang*, referring in general to the complementary aspects of nature.

Under the name of *ch'i* Chinese medicine represents the vital energy as flowing along imperceptible lines which are called meridians, and on the cutaneous envelope of the body and limbs these meridians form a network of lines of force; their existence is proved by the many senstive points to be found all along them, and they act as exterior reflexes of the whole interior organism.

For all the variety of these manifestations, one should never forget that there is only one source of energy, namely the vital Fire, mover and agent of all the operations of Nature, performing either the transmutations of generation and the coloring of the various substances, or energizing the body and all its parts with interlocking circuits of vital force.

4

Soul and Consciousness

Our habitual inexactitude in the perfunctory use of such words as "soul" and "consciousness" has meant that by now they really mean very little to those who use, read, or hear them. But a new age will need a renewed language, if only in the sense of restoring the original "spirit," the living Word, to words which have lost their meaning by too much repetition.

For one alert to its essential meaning, the properly chosen word has a magical effectiveness; but if the essential meaning is distorted, a man's whole behavior may be distorted in consequence.

Few words have been more harmfully distorted in meaning than words like "soul" and "consciousness." This is because the realities which they express are the basic elements which constitute immortal man—and which can illuminate the purpose of his existence.

Wherever the instruction of a school of initiation has been suppressed in favor of dogmas created by theological argument, the meaning of such words as "soul" and "consciousness" has always been altered to suit the prevailing fashion in religious doctrine and philosophical thinking.

In the first centuries of Christianity men spoke of the triad of body, soul, and spirit. St. Paul did not hesitate to teach that while the body of Christ was "in the tomb" his soul descended "into hell," but his spirit was "in the hands of the Father." This human triad was overtly discussed by Origen and Heraclides,* but later, after innumerable disputes among theologians, was boiled down to the obscure simplification in the Roman

*Entretien d'Origene avec Heraclide, ed. Jean Scherer (Cairo, 1949).

catechism, which states that man is composed of two elements, soul and body.

When Origen and other theologians speak of the soul as impure, wicked, or vicious, they cannot possibly refer to the "divine spark" which is the "spiritual soul." The spiritual soul is not the same as the "soul carried by the blood," which Moses forbade the Hebrews to eat with the flesh of animals. Other texts speak of the soul as situated between the spirit and the flesh, and able to gravitate either to the spirit or to the flesh; so once again there are three elements: body, soul, and spirit. This is recognized also in the Hebrew Kabbalah, which distinguishes *nefesh*, the sensitive soul whose vehicle is the blood, from *ruah*, the spirit or spiritual soul.

In every tradition of initiation the immaterial states of man have been given names to distinguish the degree of their subtlety and the extent of their immortality; but in Catholicism all these psychospiritual states are covered by one word, dangerously vague and confused: the "soul."

To express these various states each tradition naturally chose words and symbols suitable to the genius and stage of evolution of each particular race and age. To try to alter or interchange these meanings can only lead to erroneous interpretation.

Two other essential principles need to be borne in mind:

1. The laws of the past can never dictate to the present; for the experience that humanity needs can only come to it at the present moment.

2. Wisdom can work to improve the masses, but its installation in a human soul can only be realized individually.

From these two laws two conclusions follow:

First, that regarding the basic realities of the universe there must be two different forms of teaching, respectively suitable for the individual and the mass.

Second, the choice of technical terms must be made to suit the understanding of modern people.

The exactitude of a word's meaning decreases in direct proportion to its use in a demagogic manner to appeal to everyone; for the superficial mind, having no respect for the right word or the correct response, makes all notions vague, and renders discrimination impossible by its habitual acceptance of the "near-enough."

Discrimination depends on being able to distinguish between the relative and the real; but the real will only be recognized by that which is real in man, which is indestructible.

The different states of our immortal being can be described by the one word "consciousness"; but it must be understood in its essence. We shall try to make plain the different connotations of this word.

THE ORIGIN OF CONSCIOUSNESS

"Granting that there is a First Cause of the universe, this First Cause is of necessity single. But although reason compels us to accept this idea of an indivisible Unity, devoid of quantity, the comprehension of this Unity is beyond our creaturely powers as parts of the universe and effects of the single Cause. This Unity, in fact, will only exist for us if we can compare it to something; and comparison implies consciousness and duality. Therefore, creation takes place between the numbers One and Two;* and duality must be the fundamental characteristic of the created universe.

"The dualism of Nature implies comparison and the successiveness of phenomena. Unity creates by observing itself. This Unity, regarded as indivisible, may be called God or Unpolarized Energy, and regarded as self-conscious Unity it may be called God or Polarized Energy.

"Hence the universe consists of consciousness, and is nothing but the evolution of consciousness, from its beginning until it returns finally to its cause. In other words, it is evolution from an 'innate consciousness' toward a psychological conscousness, which is the awareness of innate consciousness. This is the first stage toward consciousness freed from physical contingencies, that is, the permanent and immortal consciousness.

"Man is an individual manifestation of all the functions, powers, and affinities in the universe, and his consciousness is the measure of his individualization, his power to make actual that which is still only virtual in cosmic harmony.

"Individualization gives bodily form in the organism of man to the functions of genesis, separating the creative thought in time and space; the task of our consciousness is to reunite them.

"Conscousness develops with a knowledge of the various elements of genesis and of the spiritual bond uniting them. In other words, there is knowledge of both good and evil, and also knowledge of the One; the former, comes from our mortal intelligence, which separates as a scythe, and the latter, from our immortal intelligence, which unifies."**

CONSCIOUSNESS IN THE UNIVERSE

In the beginning was the Word, and the Word was with God, and the Word was God. The same was in the beginning with God. All things were made by him; and without him was not anything made that was made. In him was life; and the life was the light of men. And the light shineth in darkness. [John 1:1-5]

---

*This again may be confirmed from the Kabbalah. (Tr. note)
**Quoted from R. A. Schwaller de Lubicz, *Le Temple dans l'Homme.*

The eternal Word, the Logos, is the potential of the Absolute. By taking substance of the cosmic Virgin, which is cosmic Consciousness or Wisdom, it became the Creative Word, the author of all things and incarnate in all.

Thus everything which enters into Becoming is an incarnation of the Creative Word. And every incarnation is a gestation which from the beginning is in darkness.

We are told that in this darkness shines the Light ''which lighteth every man that cometh into the world'' (John 1:9). This light is consciousness. And since everything in existence is thus a manifestation of the Word, a rhythm of the Word and an utterance of the Word, therefore everything in existence is a specific consciousness. And this consciousness is the innate or essential consciousness of its kind, carried by its seed, and, in a human being, enriched by the permanent consciousness of his previous experiences.

CONSCIOUSNESS IN MAN

The innate consciousness, creator of all the kingdoms of Nature, becomes in the animal kingdom the instinctual consciousness; but in man it is dormant because of his artificial education, which concentrates his attention on the evidence of his senses and his reasoning faculty. What he commonly calls consciousness is his brain-consciousness, which is only a mirror reflecting thoughts and inferences whose origin and reality he cannot clearly discern, based as they are on chance associations of ideas, impressions, and emotions.

Brain-consciousness, in other words, is only a mental projection of what a man believes himself to be, of what he believes himself to want and do, but it effectually rules him because he does not know what influences from within and without determine it, and with it his behavior; and also because brain-consciousness has no more contact with real consciousness than have two radio stations working on different wavelengths.

Without experimental knowledge of his different states of consciousness a man is controlled by his impulses, and then his free will is an illusion. And this illusion can be tragic because it can make any human being, however intelligent, an irresponsible puppet so far as his destiny is concerned. The errors that it induces are so disastrous that it is the first obstacle to be cleared out of the way if he wishes to find the real aim of his existence and not to die entirely.

At the moment of birth, the consciousness of a human individual includes the consciousness acquired during earlier experiences, grafted onto the human racial consciousness, which already includes the various forms of consciousness evolved in nature. This oversimplified explanation gives no idea of the states of consciousness of our real immortal selves; but though addressed only to the brain, it may serve to reduce the resistance of our rationalizing intelligence by showing it how to observe as a spectator the acquisition of a kind of knowledge which goes beyond it.

A trick? Yes, no doubt; but a trick which can impose an armistice on the combativeness of our reason, so that in the ensuing silence we may hear the call of our own anxiety and seek the means to awaken our real consciousness.

The Human Triad

Man has three levels of consciousness: the Automaton, Permanent Witness, the Spiritual Witness.

The Automaton is the mortal being, physical, emotional, and mental. When the mental faculties become developed, the innate or instinctive consciousness is usually put to sleep, and ceases to be perceptible by its owner; in that case he is controlled by the working of his organic functions and by the nervous, emotional, and cerebral reactions which their appetites provoke. The creature is an Automaton because it is controlled by the mutual reactions of its parts and by the exterior influences, which act upon it at every moment of its existence—influences such as country, family, relatives, education, laws, customs, and many others.

Normally, when a man has not undergone a methodical training with a view to becoming aware of his states of consciousness, they develop or atrophy unnoticed, except of course his brain-consciousness, which never allows itself to be forgotten. Thus he is controlled by his physical, mental, and emotional reactions, over which he has no check other than the explanations offered him by the five senses and the brain.

There are, however, two witnesses to the existence of this intelligent Automaton, and these are the two nonmortal states of consciousness. These two witnesses record, generally unnoticed by the Automaton, the impressions which affect it, and both provoke reactions whose origin and value are unknown to the Automaton. That there are two can be seen from the personal or impersonal quality which distinguishes the evidence they offer, and the purposes for which they offer it. We can then speak of two witnesses.

The Permanent Witness has the aspect of the personality; it has the same cycle and personal rhythm, reinforced by its inherited and astral characteristics; for the conditions of its incarnation have been determined by affinity of rhythm and by the karmic necessities of its evolution.

This witness is the Osirian element in man, and must undergo renewal through the cycles of Becoming. As such it desires the continuation of personal experience.

The Spiritual Witness has the spiritual aspect of the incarnate being, his spiritual Name, his highest form of consciousness. It represents his divine soul, or in Egyptian terms his divine *Ka*, throughout the course of his incarnations.* It is the Horus element in his evolution, because it desires to liberate him from the karmic chains of Becoming by unifying his levels of consciousness.

These two immortal witnesses correspond to the two angels which Christian tradition gives a man to advise him, the good or guardian angel and the "bad angel." The bad angel is the Permanent Witness, the permanent awareness of "I," which witnesses a man's reactions to the experiences of life and how he resists the control of his higher consciousness. Its physical center in the human body is the liver, and its listening post is in the brain.

The second is the Spiritual Witness, which is impartial because totally independent of the personality. The personality is only its vehicle of incarnation, and the object of the necessary transmutation to accomplish the task of the Christian and Horian redemption, for this redemption is attained by uniting the divine with the human. Its physical reaction center is the spleen, and its listening post is the occult center called the Spiritual Heart.

These two immortal levels of consciousness give man his advantage over the animals, and distinguish the quality of different individuals according to how one or the other predominates and according to the relations of both with the Automaton. In most human beings, unfortunately, the Automaton is the active agent, and does not even notice the existence of a continuous guiding thread.

This guiding thread is the Permanent Witness of the immortal Self. This Witness records, with or without the cooperation of the Automaton, and in a subtler medium than brain-consciousness, the results of the experiences of life. So while the Automaton is undergoing the impressions which it thinks it has created, this guiding thread pursues its intention of perfecting the type of man that it represents, by developing all the possibilities of its real Self.

The Automaton has the illusion of directing its own existence, because it has cultivated awareness of the faculties of its brain, several of which were already developed in the higher animals. This cerebral consciousness, by the comparison and association of ideas, leads it to believe that it can judge, decide, and choose.

*See Appendix II.

Thus the mortal Automaton and the immortal Self pursue their several aims beside one another, but with this difference that the Automaton is ignorant of the presence of the Self, and sometimes serves it, but more often obstructs it by inertia. In this condition man abdicates his right to be lord of Nature and the animals, for study and reason will never reveal to him the secret of life or grant him access to the supernatural realms.

That an animal should be subject to the tendencies of its species, and all their effects, is natural. It fulfills its destiny by simply following its instinctual consciousness, for the group-consciousness of its kind is the only thread of continuity which passes from one individual to another in the genes; there is no higher form of consciousness which might wish to improve the quality of the individual. It may have the qualities, or properties, of its kind accentuated more or less according to the potentialities of the genes from which it grew, but it will not be able to add any other properties to its own genetic elements. Anything which it acquires by training, outside its specific qualities, will be artificial and will not be passed on to its descendants. On the contrary, life in a state of Nature, and the difficulties which it will have to encounter in that state, will only serve to develop the instinctive qualities of its species.

In this direction the human Automaton is handicapped by its artificial education and by the mental resistance that distracts its attention from its instinctual consciousness; and so the latter atrophies for lack of use. If, however, the Automaton allows itself to be guided by its Permanent Witness, his state becomes superior to that of an animal, provided that its cerebral faculties act only as a mirror and a transcriber of experience and do not interfere by putting forward rationalizing interpretations. Thus the Permanent Witness, which is grafted onto the instinctual consciousness, can turn the Automaton into a man responsible for his conduct, and capable of learning to understand his possibilities.

This is the first step in the human but supranatural realm; for the natural man, when enlightened by this supranatural consciousness which, being immortal, becomes able by means of it to identify himself with things and beings in Nature and thus to know them and become their master.

This power, and the knowledge it gives, should be inducement enough to make anyone who has glimpsed its possibility decide to control his Automaton through the discipline of his awakened consciousness.

We are not discussing here the means of doing this, but only the possibility of doing it; one must meditate on the possibility before becoming convinced that it exists.

But the possibility has another side to it, which must be faced because it contains a serious danger, namely that, despite the advantage of awakening the Permanent Witness of a human being, the aim of this consciousness is nevertheless a selfish one, since it tends to increase the "personal" attitude.

This Permanent Witness, although immortal inasmuch as it outlasts our present existence, is still only the consciousness of a specific personal being, a specimen of the dualism of Nature. Even supposing that it should grow until it could identify itself with things and beings in Nature, and thus control them, it could not by its own power establish contact with conditions higher than its own. A man who had acquired all the powers of this level of consciousness, and has control of his Automaton, would still be held in the Osirian rhythm, which is the continuation of his personal cycle, his personal rhythm, whatever might be his designs for helping humanity.

There is thus an evident antinomy between the two witnesses. The Spiritual Witness is essentially impersonal and indifferent to the contingencies of earthly life, and so it cannot put itself at the service of a man controlled by his Permanent Witness—not that it has a different aim or a different will; what we call aim and will do not exist for the Spirit—but so great is the difference of condition and rhythm that the Permanent Witness cannot influence, modify, or even make contact with the Spiritual Witness.

On the other hand, if a man is sufficiently simple, if he makes no mental opposition to being imbued with it, then his Spiritual Witness can become incarnate in him and act through him to such an extent that his Ego-Consciousness will seem not to exist except in the manifestations of instinct. This happens with certain persons who are called "simple" or "innocent," or even "idiotic," because their rational intelligence does not interfere with their behavior, and in consequence they sometimes have moments of surprising intuition.

In fact, of course, the two witnesses are the two aspects of a single consciousness, like the two aspects of the fallen archangel: Satan, who represents Nature as separating into form, fixing and possessing, and Lucifer, whose luminous nature is attracted to its luminous Source.

The redemption of the Satanic aspect can only be achieved by "the Descent of Christ into Hell," that is to say by the experience of the Spiritual Witness descending into humanity. In this experience the two aspects become aware of each other and unite.

For this reason, however great the control obtained by one or other of the two witnesses—whether by the Personal or Permanent Witness controlling the Automaton, or by the Spiritual Witness keeping the body under control without regard to the Permanent Witness—there can be no ultimate liberation so long as one of the factors of redemption has been omitted. In the former case, the Spiritual Witness will not be there to draw the Ego out of its personal limitations and prevent it from becoming inflated. In the second, to ignore the Ego opens the door to physical maladjustments and more particularly to emotional deceptions of an imaginative (astral) or sentimental type, and these, under a semblance of divine love, may produce illusory phenomena which are obstructions in the way of spiritual realization.

In any case there can be no final liberation for any human being without attaining Unity of Consciousness, in which the Permanent Witness recognizes and accepts the guidance of the Spiritual Witness. This acceptance will obviously alter the type of control or power aimed at by the Ego, since the (higher) Self, being essentially impersonal, cannot be restricted to selfish ends.

The procedure for full realization must be as follows: first, control of the Automaton by the Permanent Witness. This will eventually produce a human being aware of the source of his impulses, conscious of his instincts and their organs, and able to see their correspondences in Nature. It is a prerequisite of success that the rational mind shall strictly limit itself to noting the results without interpreting them.

The second step is the enlargement of the Permanent Witness into the consciousness of the true Self, and for this the collaboration of the two is essential. The Spiritual Witness is there all the time; this in fact is what it has been waiting for. But the effort must be made by the Permanent Witness, in order to eliminate by continual watchfulness the various obstacles which prevent the Spiritual Witness from manifesting itself to the man now fully aware of his Permanent Witness.

The obstacles to be eliminated are selfish aims and obstinate persistence in personal points of view. If these can be removed, man becomes free to look inward and observe realities of a universal order.

5

The Aim

Our aim is to realize the suprahuman state by awakening and uniting the Permanent Witness with that of the highest Self.

The way is the conscious reanimation of the entire body, the confirmation of the interplay between its functions and all its vital reactions. It is, finally, the recognition of the several roles of the two witnesses.

Thus will be formed the milieu in which the "spiritual nucleus" will grow until it fills the entire man and generates the Incorruptible Body, of which the physical body will only be the apparent envelope and the obedient instrument.

To pursue this path without being deflected, the first requirement is the gradual destruction of automatic behavior, by learning to recognize the drama which is fought out in a human being, to know the combatants and their weapons.

This drama is the duel between the two wills, the Personal Will and the Will to the Light.

Many human beings know nothing of this drama: those whose brain-consciousness make so much noise that the two witnesses cannot be heard. In these, who are legion, the Automatic Self reigns uncontrolled, having nothing to restrain it but an atavistic moral sense and the conventional religious or social rules of its education. Moral problems, for such people, can only be a choice between obeying their established moral code and breaking it at the bidding of self-interest or instinct.

This majority is not interested in spiritual anxieties or in the Way which the present work attempts to open. The few, to whom the sages address themselves, are aware of an anxiety caused by the more or less frequent appeals of their higher consciousnesses, the Permanent Witness and the Spiritual Witness.

If the Permanent Witness is the only one to manifest, it creates a wish to gain mastery over the Automaton and act "knowingly" instead of being at the mercy of its thoughts and impulses. In such a case the mastery that can be attained will never be more than the realization of the Ego as an entity in itself, without any attempt at union with the Impersonal Self. The drama is then simply a struggle to reduce the Automaton to an obedient slave, and to gain personal powers of various kinds.

The real drama begins either when the Spiritual Witness attempts to dominate the Automaton (which leads to abnegation of the Ego and a mystical asceticism), or else when the Permanent Witness is invited by the Spiritual Witness to cooperate in realizing the suprahuman state through the supremacy of the divine impersonal element in man.

This is the beginning of the Duel, the struggle between the Personal Will and the Will to the Light.

If you allow this duel to take place, you must realize that your whole body will be the battleground. The spiritual nucleus is divine in essence, but in order to rediscover its power it must beget itself in the human heart and go through the processes of "mortification," "rebirth," and "resurrection."

It is a disastrous error to consider the soul as an ethereal Intelligence enthroned somewhere high above yourself or the world, and to think that you have to "attain" it by raising yourself on the wings of idealism and aspiration above your body and the earth.

No earthly man can perceive Spirit except in his own flesh. And this is no mere literary simile, but a most positive reality. You can only find your God by generating Him in yourself, in the darkness of your own body.

For when He takes cognizance of a substance, then He becomes its God.

This substance can have no God but its own, when once it has become His cradle and His Temple.

"There is no God but God," and no Light but the Word; but each creature can know only its own Word; and the Father of Light is unknowable and inaccessible to those who have not learned to partake of His oneness.

The Height must penetrate the Depth, if you wish the Depth to become as the Height, "to accomplish the miracle of the One Thing," as says the Emerald Table.

But since there are Depth and Height, neither can be moved without the other, and they depend upon each other.

"And the Light [of the Word] shineth in darkness."

Certain timid persons deny Its Presence in abject places and manure as a sacrilegious idea. But the blasphemy lies in such doubt. To the Spirit nothing is unclean save those who reject It. The vilest filth can accept the Spirit, but rational thought and the Ego-Witness can reject it because each of them can imagine that it is itself the Light.

If you desire the Light, be sure that you will never find it except by begetting it in your own darkness. Do not blaspheme by calling it incompatible with the darkness of matter; for matter would not exist if the Light were not already formed within it.

And this Light, so soon as awakened, will become your Master, full of power, your God dwelling in you, who transforms all effort into joy, all storms into exaltation, all mysteries and doubts into Knowledge.

Only beware not to remain in indecision. Have the courage to sound your depths and choose your path. Halfheartedness and compromise can only lead to useless suffering.

6

The Duel

To understand the two actors in the duel, a great deal of thought is needed. For one actor is simple, immaterial, and only to be recognized by the "intelligence of the heart"; but the other is so complicated that only the closest introspection can analyze it.

By "intelligence of the heart" we must understand that form of mental activity which begins with the reawakening, deliberate or not, of the occult center between the heart and solar plexus. This center is the Spiritual Heart.

The first actor to appear in us as a will toward the Light is our own spiritual Logos, the voice of our divine *Ka,* the spiritual observer of our human experience.

Its apparent function is to provide the impulse which obliges us to determine our conduct from a higher motive than mere egoism. When this impulse has been accepted, its real function will be to activate our occult centers, intuitive and spiritual. The result will be the sense of a real Presence which calms anxieties and takes away our painful sense of uncertainty and impotence.

The second actor, which does the real fighting by resisting the impersonal self, is the Personality as a whole, that is to say the Automaton with its physical, emotional, and cerebral components, plus the Ego-Consciousness, its Permanent Witness.

It must be clearly understood that everything in us which is neither the Permanent Witness nor the Spiritual Witness is part of the Automaton. The movements of the organism belong to it, both voluntary and autonomic, so do the thoughts, acts, and decisions directed by the will and consciousness of the brain; for these depend on the organism (the physical, emotional, and mental) and are therefore mortal, as it is.

To arouse oneself from the state of sleep and take the first step toward liberation, one must attain a thorough understanding of the meaning of the Permanent Witness (or Ego-Consciousness) and see in what it differs from mere brain-consciousness.

We shall then be able to understand how this personal conscience, though it needs to be awakened, is nevertheless a part of the Personality whose aims are in general opposed to those of the Spiritual Self.

The Personality wants:

• Continuity on earth
• The relative values of this temporary existence
• Intellectual information put at the service of worldly interests (a social, scientific, or commercial career)
• Mediocrity—since rash extremes can never expect to win public approval and gain social and worldly advantages
• Utilitarianism, meaning everything that fits in with mundane computations and logical reason.

The Spiritual Witness, on the other hand, desires:

• To unite with the human and thus transmute it into an immortal being
• Absolute values, which are indestructible
• To open the ''heart'' to intuitive knowledge
• The sense of excess, as a springboard from which to overleap human limitations and convert the fall of man into an opportunity of evolution
• Unalterable love of Reality
• Love of life for its own sake
• Love of Impersonal Love.

The Personality wills only itself, and each of its constituent parts defends only its own existence. When the Automaton is not controlled by the Permanent Witness, it is guided by nothing beyond its own brain-consciousness, and this, as we have seen already, is just a mental projection of what it supposes itself to be and to want; in consequence it is ruled by the various impulses aroused by its dominant instincts, or by outside influences, and this anarchy leads to psychic and organic disorders. If it does receive any suggestions from the Permanent Witness, it attributes them to its own intellectual decision, not knowing how to differentiate.

The greatest difficulty is to distinguish between the Ego of the intelligent animal Automaton and the conscious Ego of the Permanent Witness. For even in altruistic actions, unless inspired by the Spiritual Witness, the aims of both are personal; the Automaton carries them out to satisfy its animal, sentimental, or rational impulses, and the Permanent

Witness devises them in order to gain its personal ends. For the Ego is never altruistic at its own expense; it cannot seek to lose itself. Abnegation and the longing for the impersonal come from the Spiritual Witness. The cunning of the Ego in diverting them to its own advantage is positively devilish.

The most common trap is a matter of the words "I" and "me," which create confusion between the automatic "I," with its various selves, and the conscious "I." To penetrate this false Ego we must learn the full repertory of its disguises—its professional ego, its social ego, its sexual ego, its pious or skeptical ego, and its ego for family use; they all have different faces, characters, and behavior, according to their several ages, circumstances, and secret passions. But each of these "me's" says "I want" and "I promise," pretending not to know that one of the other "I's" may contradict it.

To be more precise, this is not a mere disagreement over meanings of words; rather one must become one's own confessor in order to be no longer deceived by that undiscoverable mirage of a character, the multiple "I" of daily life. First, one of its disguises appears, then another, according to the role that has to be played, but all are recorded in the mirror of the Akasha,* which is the mirror of judgment.

Now judgment presupposes a judge and a thing judged, and here it indicates two conditions, the original consciousness and the newly acquired consciousness. This judgment is not a temporal event; rather it happens at every moment whenever the conscious Self becomes aware of the images projected by its Personality, and cannot any longer consent to be identified with the Personality. That is the moment of true contrition, the moment when an expansion of consciousness makes it possible to gauge the true value of an act. Final liberation occurs only when the two consciousnesses become united, and then the past becomes a part of the Becoming.

The first step toward liberation is to get rid of confusion, and this means measuring words against their meanings, and appearances against realities. We shall, however, avoid the methods of psychoanalysis and dissociation, which are new traps invented by the intellectual ego to increase its own importance.

If our final aim is simple, the way to it should be simple too. So let us ask a simple question: "I" is the word which exists to specify the agent who speaks, thinks, or acts, but does it always refer to the same "I" or agent? No, only to one of the aspects of the "Self." That being so, we had better agree that, in the present study, the word "I" shall be used to signify the total "self" of the Automaton, which, under whatever aspect,

*See Appendix II.

undergoes what it supposes itself to do or to will freely—for it has no consciousness other than brain-consciousness, the consciousness of the real self being not yet active or awakened.

The meaning given here to the words "I," "Self," and "Ego" is not simply a personal choice between the different philosophical concepts of their meanings, and the degree of reality and permanence which these concepts grant or deny to the Ego. On the contrary, the words are used here in a way designed to distinguish the different aspects of the human Automaton from our permanent consciousness which is the witness of our successive life experiences.

The word "I" does not easily take on this double meaning. Its common unthinking use does make it hard to remember a distinction, which in any case we are apt to overlook. In common usage "I" represents the person speaking of himself at the moment, referring to the states, acts, and functions of his Automaton; necessarily therefore it implies the totality of these, and refers indifferently to any of them. That accordingly is the meaning to be given to it here.

The word "Self"* has here two applications:

1. It may refer to the various single aspects of the Personality which describes itself as "I." These different selves are roles acted by the Automaton in response to the suggestion of the moment—impermanent characters, each of which thinks itself entitled to say "I am the self."

2. We call the Conscious Self, on the other hand, the Permanent Witness, individual and immortal, representing an innate and permanent reality, which, however, can evolve. It is innate because it is incarnate in us at birth, and permanent because it is the consciousness we have acquired by experience through the long series of phases of our becoming; but it can evolve because it enriches itself with every new experience of life.

Since this Permanent Witness can evolve, it is not unalterable; this quality can only be attributed to the spiritual element, "divine soul," or "divine *Ka*," of which we have knowledge only through the impulses of that higher consciousness which is the Spiritual Witness. That is the true Self, but here is not the place for vain discussion about its reality and survival, on which metaphysicians have many points of view.

Here we shall speak of that consciousness which is "of" the Universal Consciousness, but innate and particularized in every human being, asleep in some, but awakened in others who enrich it by their experience and by their specific character. This is called here the Permanent Witness, or Personal Consciousness.

We shall speak also of the same Universal Consciousness in its impersonal and therefore divine state, but this is the Spiritual Witness,

*Moi. (Trans. note)

which desires to enlighten the Permanent Witness and, by uniting with it, redeem it from its contact with the dualism of Nature and restore it to its original state.

These are the realities; call them by what names you will, one thing is certain: This double form of consciousness is our immortal element, the subject on which all the "emissaries of heaven" have preached, the unique treasure which gives value to human existence, the one imperishable possession to be preserved. These realities, proclaimed unanimously by the sages, will surely suffice to decide for us the aim of human life; and to choose a path which accords with human possibilities is better than the chancy pursuit of an ineffectual ideal.

What is the use of speculating on states of supreme beatitude, or ecstatic meditation in the highest *samadhi,* if our present state of consciousness can offer us no knowledge of them? The earth is only one stage of our pilgrimage, and we must gather our experience with the means at our disposal on earth. If lofty beings have attained to ecstatic communion with the unknowable, their evidence only confirms the possibility of such a thing, and shows that divine beatitude can be known by their Spiritual Witness, which has returned to tell of it.

This testimony is confirmed by their serene certainty, by the radiance of their Reality, which may arouse the spiritual hunger of others and show them glimpses of the path. Their experience, however, cannot be used as a pattern for others to follow; experience must always be individual, and self-knowledge, which is the indispensable foundation, can only be attained by individual effort.

THE TWO STAGES OF THE DUEL

The duel is fought first of all between the Automaton and the Permanent Witness, the latter trying to impose on the automatic "I" a style of behavior which will enable it to bring its inherent nature to fulfillment. This can be exemplified by conscious control of the organic functions, gestures, and psychological reactions; refusal to follow inherited patterns, habits, and prejudices; observation of what tendencies are genuinely one's own; and conscious control over the subconscious and unconscious. The program of these requirements of the Permanent Witness is quite a task in itself, and will be analyzed further on.*

The aim of the struggle between the automatic "I" and the Personal Self is to bring about the fulfillment of this program. For this self shows what it wants, by putting forward suggestions and impulses to the Automaton, who disputes their suitability and tries to evade them. Then

*See Chapters 15 and 16.

the Personality must plead the attractions of personal advantage, spectacular powers, impressive superiority, or simply a high professional reputation.

This cultivation of the personal self can have a certain value, but it will only serve to exalt the Ego so long as the Ego has sole control.

This nevertheless is the first victory we must win, in order to subject the automatic "I" to the control of the conscious "I," and put brain-consciousness at the service of the Permanent Witness, so that the latter, out of its earlier experience, can rectify the data provided by the computations of thinking.

The first result will be to arouse the Automaton from its slumber, and the second will be to give an unsuspected interest to the problems of daily life—the interest which a trainer takes in controlling a wild beast, or a mountaineer in climbing inaccessible peaks—the interest that comes of knowing the inclinations and secret aim of one's personality, and how to work for their realization by methods of one's choice.

Here we have two possibilities: Either we can enjoy a sporting interest in the struggle, keenly intent on the glorification of the Ego, or else we can regard the result as a first awakening from sleep and the acquisition of the technique which later on will enable us to subject the Personal Consciousness to control by the Spiritual Witness. In the same way a mountaineer, having climbed a dangerous peak, instead of reveling in a sportsman's pride, might find in the exaltation of the heights an opportunity to forget his personal limitations and make contact with the Impersonal.

But that which seems easy on the luminous heights becomes more tiresome in the banal conditions of the daily round. And the Permanent Witness demands the just reward of its victory.

For this reason it is imprudent to push too far this cultivation of the Personal Self, or leave it in sole command of the situation. As soon as the first successes have been obtained, it should be subjected to competition from the Spiritual Witness.

In this second phase of the duel the Automaton will be apt to side with its master, the Personal Self, and help it to resist the suggestions of the Spiritual Self.

The latter, however, does not use the practical methods of the Personal Self; rather it acts by insinuation, alternating between flashes of light and dark silence, until one becomes dissatisfied and longs urgently for its presence.

The battle is now no longer between the brain, the liver, the sex, and their allies; the heart alone must undertake by its own serenity to resist their revolts. If the Will to the Light can achieve the transfer of authority to the physical and spiritual heart, the heart will prove that by its pacifying power it can establish equilibrium in the organism and bring about a state of peace in which the aggressive claims of the Personality will gradually diminish.

The possibility of this second kind of control will be studied when we have described the practical means of attaining the first, which is control by the Permanent Witness.

The heart draws its strength from participation in the Impersonal, to which it opens by giving itself, by expansion and nonresistance.

It seems illogical that the cooperation of the conscious Ego can be obtained in the work of regeneration which is going to destroy its egotism. What makes this possible is the contagious joy which emanates from the presence of the Spiritual Witness; for its presence arouses the "Intelligence of the Heart," and the Knowledge that results has an attraction for the Personal Self, because if it agrees to use its ability more and more in the service of the Impersonal, it will be able in return for its sacrifice to share this Knowledge and enjoy immortal union with the Spiritual Witness.

THE TWO KEYS TO THE SUPRAHUMAN REALM

Access to the Kingdom of Heaven is symbolized in the Christian church by two keys, the silver key and the golden key. In Egypt it was symbolized by the two crowns, the white crown and the red crown.

This double symbol of perfection represents the highest condition of humanity, the suprahuman state, which is accessible to man on earth through the awakening of his higher levels of consciousness, followed by gradual regeneration of the human through the divine.

The silver key stands for temporal power over beings and states of being which are part of Nature. It is temporal in the sense of being conditioned by the time and circumstances of their becoming. The golden key stands for the power of the Spiritual Witness allied to its universal divine principle. The two keys together represent the indissoluble union of the consciously divine and the consciously human, which is the realization of Christhood.

The difference of the two powers is shown by Christ's words to Peter: "...thou savorest not the things that be of God, but the things that be of men" (Mark 8:33).

The silver key corresponds to the white crown of Osiris, the *Neter* (or principle) of existential becoming, by which life vanishes into death only to be reborn in another form.

Osiris is the Lord of Nature and rules its functions, which are the multitudinous incarnations of consciousness. According to the Egyptian teaching the Osiris in man is the Personal Consciousness, his Permanent Witness, and in the afterlife remains in the kingdom of Osiris, which during its life on earth it has learned to rule.

This afterlife, be it noted, is a relative, not an ultimate, immortality. It is a posthumous state corresponding to what could be called a transitory "earthly paradise," as suggested by the Greek word *paradeisos,* meaning a park, garden, or orchard; for although not subject to the contingencies of physical existence it does represent a psychically vegetative state, and was presented as such in ancient mythology (the Elysian Fields of Greece, the Egyptian Field of Reeds, Muhammad's Garden of Paradise, and so forth). These pictures refer to terrestrial attachments contracted through personal desires and aims.

The state is transitory because its duration is determined by the more or less rapid exhaustion of its attractions (of the thirst for it, in Egyptian terms), or else by the need for a new incarnation.

The Osirian Consciousness is that of the Permanent Witness, and gives man on earth the key to control his three lower states of being (the physical, psychic, and mental) and the three corresponding worlds or states in his own universe.

But this degree of mastery is only the lower level of the suprahuman kingdom; it still refers to "the things of men," and not at all to "the things of God." The spiritual cannot be attained by the Personal Consciousness until it allows itself to be transcended by the Spiritual Witness.

The golden key corresponds to the red crown and the spiritual power which is conferred by consciousness of the divine. This key gives what is needed to attain the higher degree of the suprahuman realm, namely the radiance of the spiritual heart.

When the red crown, or spiritual consciousness, is united to the white crown, or personal consciousness purified of its egoism, it is called "the double power" (*sekhemti*), and this is the supreme power of completed consciousness which gives ultimate immortality.

In the human body the spiritual heart and its minister, the physical heart, hold the golden key to the divine realm where the Spiritual Witness is at home.

Gold as a symbol signifies the perfection of the mineral realm, the complementary ingredients being indissolubly combined, hence the cessation of antagonisms and the perfection of a kingdom.

Just as the physical heart receives the blood with its white and red corpuscles, pure or vitiated, and controls the circuit in which they are regenerated, so too, if we watch carefully and submit to the control of the spiritual heart the decisions of the Ego and the impressions of lower states of consciousness, the spiritual heart will be able to alter their character and tendency just as the sun matures the color and taste of fruit. It will be able to do this provided that we do not allow the Ego to stand in the way with its exclusive egocentricity.

The two keys are acquired in different ways. Mastery of the Permanent Witness is obtained by the practical methods to be described in Chapters 15 and 16.

To awaken the radiance of the spiritual heart depends on our inner disposition and on the purification of our inner environment. The program for achieving this may be called the Way of the Heart.

PART TWO

7
The Way of the Heart

When considering the Duel we decided that the combatants were two aspects of oneself, the conscious "I" or Permanent Witness, and the automatic "I," which refuses to be controlled. But the submission of the conscious "I" to the fleeting suggestions of the "Will to the Light" soon awakens the Spritiual Witness, but we must learn to know the way leading to it.

This Way we have called "the Way of the Heart" because upon it the Heart, in its physical and spiritual totality, is lord and master. This is the royal road because it gives all the power to the Spritual Witness of the king within, the divine *Ka*. It is the way of the "little children" to whom the Kingdom of Heaven is promised, because it is the simple way, without intellectual complications or artifical methods, which awakens our innate consciousness and enlarges it into a suprahuman consciousness by following obediently the suggestions of the heart.

Yet this simplicity does not mean the end of the Duel, nor yet of the need for the awakening of the Permanent Witness. Even the last phase of our evolution on earth will not allow us to skip this stage, for it must be reached in order to realize the plenitude of human earthly experience, that being the aim of our incarnation. And the conditions of incarnation never put impassible obstacles in the way of that realization. The obstacles are to be used without rancor as providential opportunities to break our chains.

We can, of course, endeavor to improve our conditions, and we shall succeed to the extent that our efforts are guided by our Will to the Light. Our Spiritual Witness cannot feel pity for the trials of our Personality; rather it will increase them, in order to hasten our deliverance—unless we deliberately silence it, in which case it would leave us forever and we should lose our real immortality.

On the other hand, when our ultimate goal is clearly seen and accepted, one is usually surprised to see the circumstances of life spontaneously alter as if to fit in with the new direction.

THE MIDDLE WAY

The Way to be studied here is a middle way between the quest for human mastery on the part of the conscious ''I'' and the pure mystical way, which no longer concerns itself with this ''I.''

When a man has trained his ''I,'' or Permanent Witness, to control his Automaton, he may develop his physical, emotional, and intellectual consciousness so well that he acquires various powers in these three realms; but these, though useful in an earthly sense, are an obstacle to spiritual realization, because they conduce to the exaltation of the personal Ego, which will take entire control if the Will to the Light is not developed at the same time; and then, should any feeling arise of desire for a higher kind of life, there will be no way of responding to this desire, and confusion will result.

If, on the other hand, one plunges into a quest for mystical experience without the precaution of studying the Personal Self and controlling the Automaton, one will unwittingly become their slave and expose oneself to organic disorders as well as intellectual and emotional delusions. One will also be rejecting the highest experience that humanity can at present know, namely, complete knowledge of the self or microcosm, which by enlargement of consciousness leads to the suprahuman state.

The aim of the middle way is first to awaken the conscious being which slumbers in the Automaton, and then to put into his hand the two keys of the kingdom, which are first the control of the three lower states, and then their use in the service of the Spiritual Self. Neither key should be used without the other, and in this the heart acts as mediator, since it is both the regulator of the physical organism and the minister of the Spiritual Witness.

If one wishes the heart to predominate, one must know the strength and methods of its antagonist, and then instead of a duel there will be a competition between the powers of the heart and liver. For the heart does not fight; it gives suggestions and tries to establish peace and harmony, which the liver, with its will to exclusive control, resists.

As was said above, the character and functions of the liver are complex. It has three lobes with three different functions, and thus it forms with the gallbladder a fourfold group of organs as important as the other fourfold group consisting of stomach, spleen, and pancreas together with the heart, which works with them in the distribution of energy.

The left-side group can be called the cardiac group, and the right-side group the hepatic group, and their functions are parallel, thus holding them in balance against one another.

The action of the liver on the blood corpuscles is paralleled by that of the spleen, and there is a parallel between the emotional characters of the two organs and the moral effects of their activity. The liver holds the seed of the Ego, with its innate characteristics inherited from the father. The spleen is the seat of the impulses and of the etheric body, inherited from the mother, and is the organ which responds to the Spiritual Witness.

The liver, in spite of its Jupiterian amiability, produces the bile, which is bitter and separative. The moral effect of the activity of the bile is either courage and daring or else anger and aggression, according to whether it acts properly or defectively. In the same way the emotion derived from the spleen may be either exalting or depressing, according to whether it derives from a spiritual impulse or an organic deficiency.

In both cases, therefore, there are two possible reactions, an automatic reaction or a conscious reaction. With the liver the reaction is either instinctive, involving the brain and bile, or else a deliberate reaction of the Permanent Witness. With the spleen there is either an instinctive reaction, violent, impulsive, and splenetic, or else a deliberate reaction by the Spiritual Witness.

If the spleen is irritated by the bile-brain circuit, unpleasant emotion will result, which will react on the solar plexus, then return to the bile, and so forth.

In the cardiac group, the heart is never on the side of the Automaton. If the bile circuit has not been cut, the heart will be mechanically affected by disturbances, but it responds to the aggression of its enemies with nonresistance, merely restoring the balance and repairing the damage.

It is just as if two kings were sharing the government of a kingdom, each discharging the functions for which he is fitted, but using their influence in exactly opposite ways. In the ''hepatic government'' the liver is chief minister for the Automaton and sometimes also for the Conscious Self, in which case it often becomes a battleground between the two. It also extends its rule over the two poles of the human body, the cerebral and the sexual. In the ''cardiac government,'' on the other hand, the heart is never an instigator of trouble. Unlike its egocentric antagonist, it subserves the general harmony, being the minister of the spiritual heart, which is the seat of spiritual love.

THE POWER OF THE HEART

Thus, even in its physical functions, the heart is genuinely the organ of peace. But, not being under the control of the Personal Will and the intellectual faculties, its decisive role is commonly misunderstood and most people consider it only a machine, thus depriving it of its opportunities.

Without knowing its extraordinary power one cannot give the heart the preponderant influence it should have. An experienced cardiologist writes:

> The kingdom of the heart, including its channels of distribution in the blood vessels, covers the full extent of any living being both in time and space. The heart is engaged in the mysterious work of holding the whole organism in balance, which is more than a matter of blood vessels and changing pressures. To correct the effects of injury or disequilibrium it has remarkable methods of compensation justified by thousands of years of experience. This Wisdom of the Heart has come to us by heredity, as a quality of our species. The heart possesses an ability to repair damage affecting itself without for one moment interrupting the flow of energy it provides. Thus it is rightly a symbol of unfailing generosity. In the practice of cardiology we have had to recognize that the heart's power to maintain life is almost unlimited, so long as it is allowed to use its own methods and has unrestricted access to its natural resources. [Here the author makes a reservation regarding "situations which are beyond mechanical control, such as a massive embolism of the pulmonary artery, when the heart fails because the task is practically impossible.] Only too frequently, however, the unfortunate interventions of the psyche, especially in the form of anxiety, turn the course of events into catastrophe. A strong heart, very little damaged, has often been known to fail in a few hours under the influence of acute anxiety. One emotional storm can demolish completely the marvelous structure of homoeostatic defenses which, with the Wisdom of the Heart, has come down to us from the depths of time.*

The experience of this tried cardiologist confirms our statement of the heart's strength of reaction when attacked by illness, and also of its ability to repair vascular lesions, if a serene and confident disposition allows it to act unhindered.

Further, being closely involved with the organs of its own region (the spleen, pancreas, and stomach), it can either compensate their functional disorders or else become the victim of them, according to one's mental and emotional attitude. If one can achieve complete physical and moral relaxation, and perform one calming "mediation" on the region of the heart, then the heart will be able to exercise its curative power freely. But its power can be checkmated either by such drugs as prevent the organism from defending itself by its natural reactions, or equally by an anxious mental analysis of pathological symptoms.

To practice the middle way it is indispensable to know the powers of the

---

*Dr. Godel, *L'Experience liberatrice* (Paris: Gallimard, 1952), p. 124.

heart, since its influence must predominate. This Way is a continual balance between the egoism of the Personal Self and the altruism of the Spiritual Self. Only the heart can achieve this wonderful act of balance, by its mediating position between the temporal and the extratemporal, between the mortal organism and its immortal archetype. Its alternating movement of dilation and contraction is a complete picture of this balance between the two powers, of which the personal must become conscious in order then to be transcended by the impersonal.

We must therefore always remember these two objectives:

First, by constant vigilance, we have to arouse our Personal Consciousness, in order that it in turn may enlighten our brain-consciousness regarding the origin of our impulses, in the realm of thought no less than of feeling. Second, and at the same time, we must become aware, through the practice of "mediation," of the interplay of our organic functions, being careful however to avoid any medical or psychoanalytic pattern of thought.

Yet as soon as the conscious "I" is aroused, it must be put under control of the Spiritual Consciousness, and not allowed to use its power for selfish ends. Like a sporting dog, it must be trained to flush the game, but not to hunt for its own enjoyment.

If the Ego is to make this sacrifice, it must be offered some compensation, and the compensation can only be a satisfaction superior to its own little selfish satisfactions; it will in fact be the increasing Light which illumines each new step along the path. It will be the enthusiasm which comes with each awakening of true Knowledge; with the successive breaking of chain after chain until at last the Ego's own shell is broken when the continuous presence of the Spirit has overcome its last resistance and drawn it into the Light.

The quickest way of attaining this is the frequent practice of "mediation" on the heart.

MEDIATION OF THE HEART

This consists of quietly concentrating attention on the heart and the region between the heart and solar plexus, which is the physical correspondence of the Spiritual Heart; for there is the true tabernacle of the Divine Presence whose temple is the human body. It should be the focus of our careful attention, in order that we may be able to hear the voice of our Spiritual Witness, and maintain the vital Fire.

This feeling of the Presence will become a force helping us to overcome all sorts of obstacles, if we constantly intensify it by "mediation."

This "mediation," or meditation on the Spiritual Heart, should begin with an intense effort to identify one's own heart with the Heart of the

Cosmos, which is our source of light and life, the focus and principle of all affinity.

Next, one must let oneself be penetrated by the peacemaking power of one's own physical and spiritual heart, and by confidence in it allow it to have its full effect. This is in no way a matter of autosuggestion or imagination, but rather of identification or direct communion with reality.

Third, one must put aside all feelings of anxiety, rancor, and pessimism, which would prevent any such communion.

This is essential because there can be no communion between rhythms or tendencies which are opposed to one another. The heart's tendency is to make peace by establishing such a rhythm as will compensate any unbalance; and the cause of this tendency is the Spiritual Heart, of which the physical organ is the physical expression. Any disposition to obstruct this tendency is an obstruction to the appearance of the Presence, because it creates discord instead of communion. So every time a feeling of aggressiveness or anxiety is overcome, the heart has won a useful victory over its opponents—useful because this is the way to the Light.

Thanks to this practice the complications of daily life lose their importance, problems become simpler, and difficulties melt away in proportion as one becomes more able to know the real from the relative and discern the few things really necessary.

This mediation on the heart is the keystone of the middle way, the only method that we can offer as genuinely effective, and not requiring, as other practices do, an instructor to make sure of its proper execution.

Further, this middle way does not require any of the complicated exercises of Yoga, which are dangerous unless practiced under an experienced teacher. As for the methods designed to develop the supremacy of the Ego, to win power and assert the will, they are a great deal worse.

On the Way of the Heart the first difficulty is the simplicity of the method, for our modern minds, being trained in complication, cannot believe that a simple method will be effective. For this reason many seekers prefer the doubtful procedures of more spectacular methods.

But "simple" does not mean "easy," even when, as here, it implies simple-heartedness and a simple technique.

Simplicity of instruction is meant to keep the aim clear, to prevent unnecessary detours and involvements.

Simplicity of thought is exclusion of the irrelevant.

Simplicity of heart means detachment from that which is not essential to our aim, detachment from our previous intellectual riches, prejudices, opinions, and beliefs, thus leaving us free to undertake the quest of Reality with the ingenuous open-heartedness of a child looking upon the world with new eyes.

Why should this abnegation fill us with anxiety? The more the heart is an avid void, the more abundantly will the Light shine into it. And as for the scientific knowledge which we temporarily leave aside, its essential principles will only be made clearer by our greater discernment.

But no one will oblige us to perform these acts of renunciation. There is no law, no commandement, no "Thou shalt not." The inner voice will suggest to us what sacrifices are necessary.

There can be nothing unspontaneous on this path. Only the limit of our desire will be the limit of our progress.

8

The Fountain

There is only one fountain—the eternal Wisdom—and its messenger is the Spirit with its seven gifts.

This is the rainbow bridge between heaven and earth, which reveals the seven colors of the one Light.

Every man can receive this light, in the color that his own prism refracts.

And there is only one Knowledge—the knowledge of the laws of genesis.

This Knowledge can be understood under diverse forms and divided into different branches: the science of numbers, entities, and universal functions; the science of phases, or transformations, in any kind of genesis; the science of natures, characters, and their signatures. Each of these branches can be the fountain of several human sciences, but all are aspects of the one Knowledge, which is that of genesis. It is the foundation of the first book of Moses, as of all sacred books.

Mystical knowledge, or the science of the genesis of the mystic Egg, is no different; it is the knowledge of the becoming of the heavenly man within the earthly man, and of the regeneration of the earthly man by the heavenly man. We say knowledge rather than science because it is not indispensable to have studied its laws before attaining it in oneself; a sudden illumination may awaken the spiritual seed in one who is so disposed. And one who is absolutely docile to the guidance he receives can bring this seed to maturity in full consciousness, by a perpetual circuit of communion between the seed and its Cause.

The foundation must not be sought in those complicated theologies which at a later time have been grafted onto originally genuine revelations.

The nearer the front, the briefer is the teaching of truth; for the laws which it is vitally necessary to know can be expressed in few words.

Of essential truths there are more packed into the Book of Genesis than in all the rest of the Old Testament. More splendid perhaps, because even more condensed, is the Emerald Tablet of Hermes, which teaches in a few words the great unitary law of the identity of "that which is above" with "that which is below"; and this is the whole teaching of Ancient Egypt.

In the same way the first lines of the Gospel of John tell a man all that he needs to know to find his way. For when a man has recognized and proved upon himself that in the beginning of anything there is always the Word, that all things live by It, that Its life is Light, and that the gestation of this Light is in darkness, then he knows that his true aim is to awaken and bear this light in the darkness of his body, until its resurrection is complete.

But to reveal Truth to another is a thing no one can pretend. One's only instructor is oneself.

A book or a Master may point out the predispositions necessary in order to find Truth; but to explain it is to kill understanding in advance.

No Master worthy of the name can deceive himself by claiming to impose a new belief. All he can do is help seekers to understand the teaching of the sages, so far as they can at the present stage of their awareness.

No new truths await discovery; everything has been given already. But it has all been scattered abroad and dispersed, misrepresented by analysis, dulled by routine repetition. The essential words have been prostituted.

We must recover the vital meaning of these ideas.

9
Knowledge

Knowledge is not a science but a state—the state of identification. To be identified with something is to be united with it and made one with it.

Identification can take place only between states of being of the same type, but these, like liquids of the same density, will interpenetrate naturally; thought communicates with thought, emotion with emotion, and passion with passion of the same kind, and this is why, between individuals or groups, thought, emotion, and passion can be communicated without words.

No individual can communicate with another on a "wavelength" which the latter does not possess. For example, a man cannot transmit a moral, intellectual, or religious emotion to an animal, since the latter cannot vibrate, as it were, on that wavelength. A wild creature, when it meets a traveler, knows by instinct whether his intentions toward it are friendly or aggressive, because it has such feelings itself; but it will pick up the emotional or passional condition of the man, not his thought or reasoning or plan of attack. The man, on the other hand, can use his reasoning power to guess at the intentions of the animal, but he will rarely understand its feelings because his own mental activity prevents him from communicating with it on that level.

Knowledge is thus the state of identification with a condition or a function.

Now, function is a particular modality of consciousness. Every species in Nature is characterized by certain functions and modalities which constitute its innate or instinctive consciousness. This instinctive consciousness is, for an animal, its "knowledge," that is to say, its state of being identified with the conditions and functions of its kind.

This direct knowledge is different from the intellectual apprenticeship of learned knowledge, which comes from the exercise of observation, memory, deduction, and technique. The newborn kitten, though blind, suckles by the light of Nature; it is identified with a function of its kind, and this it knows directly: but, later on, the place where the saucer of milk is put will have to be learned.

The bounds of knowledge are much wider in man, because he possesses the elements, or at least the listening posts, of higher states than the physical, emotional, and mental. For these higher states are the projection in the human being of the same states of being in the Cosmos.

Identification, however, is more difficult for man than for an animal, because the egocentricity of his Personal Consciousness (the Permanent Witness) prevents him from wanting to be identified with anything but himself, and equally because the rational mind restricts the Automaton to the rational way of using the mind, and will not allow it to tune in to any mode of thought superior to its own. (For "mode of thought" we might say "vibrations"; all this is metaphor.)

The identification most commonly in force is that of the Automaton with its lower states (the physical, emotional, and intellectual), while the Permanent Witness remains inactive except for a general urge toward anything that can inflate the Ego. When this happens, the impressions derived from each of the three lower states are vaguely felt by the other two, so that physical pains and other sensations become confused with emotions, and judgments or opinions are given under the influence of an exhilaration or depression which is of physical or emotional origin.

This confusion controls the individual's behavior. Neither of the two real forms of consciousness (the Personal or the Spiritual) can throw any light upon it because he would not hear them if they spoke, and he has no studied principle whereby to classify impressions according to their causes. Neither the Permanent nor the Spiritual Witness can interfere with this chaos of impressions because its principles (or its "wavelength") are different from theirs.

They cannot, that is, except by provoking some violent shock which will surprise the Automaton into contact with one of the two witnesses before the rational mind has time to react. This contact gives the Automaton an impression of light and vital force, which, vitally, it will want to find again; and this is why a sudden moral or spiritual transformation sometimes occurs after a violent emotion, a serious illness, or an escape from death.

These shocks are a means frequently employed by one or the other witness-consciousness to shake the Automaton out of its lethargy and take the rational mind by surprise. One must not forget that this proceeding, by the repetition of suitable shocks, can eventually keep the Automaton under the control of one of its witnesses. The choice between these, and indeed the possibility of such a thing at all, are to be illustrated in the present work. Its object is to awaken man from his mortal slumber and put his Automaton into the service of the two witnesses in such manner and measure as shall be required for the attainment of ultimate deliverance. The result should be an acquisition of true knowledge, which will naturally be proportionate to the quality of the consciousness awakened and to the degree of identification.

All functions and states of being can become objects of Knowledge. The innate human consciousness includes all the functional consciousnesses which are the framework of Nature; for, man being the microcosm of the macrocosm, all states of being in the Cosmos are projected in him. In other words, he has in himself all the possibilities of Knowledge, and it is in himself that he should look for them.

Not even the best teacher can present one with consciousness, or fill one with knowledge; but in a man suitably disposed it is possible to arouse reactions which will lead in the right direction.

Often it is useful to prepare the ground by clarifying essential ideas in order to get rid of prejudices. But the most effective instruction is that which leads the seeker to put his problems clearly to himself so that then he can find the answer for himself in meditation.

Here we shall try to practice alternately the two methods, explanation and stimulation, trusting that the reader will accept our meditative reflections as the somewhat simple method, in fact the simplest possible method, of gradually approaching that simplicity of heart and mind to which the Kingdom of Heaven has been promised.

Here there is no longer any author or reader; there is, or let us hope there is, only Consciousness. And the Consciousness of I and You is, let us hope, a little piece of the Universal Consciousness—unless indeed it is only an elucubration of my thinking brain, which pretends to be Myself. How can I tell?

That which I think I know is that which my thought has recognized as evidential; but it has sometimes happened that certain evidence has been impugned by later scientific discovery.

This "Myself" which thinks it understands is an activity of the brain. The Myself which thinks it wills may be the impulse of some urge of passion or of some unrecognized mental suggestion. And the Myself which thinks it loves has loved so many different things that I doubt whether it is always the same itself. "I" might doubt? Who then is this "I"? Who asks this question? Who is speaking now? Is it that "I" have doubts about

"Myself," or does "I" doubt "It"? Is "I" "Myself"? If it were, how could it be ignorant of "Myself's" intentions? And if "Myself" were to die now, would "I" be still there asking, "Who am I?"

Discussion cannot solve this problem. "I" accuses the incoherent "Myself" of not revealing the motives of its behavior. Sometimes it thinks as "I" thinks, sometimes it does what "I" does not like, and its acts are inconsistent, as if there were several "Me's" acting at their own whims or under some outside influence.

But to be able to take note of this seems to give "I" an advantage over the multifarious "Myself"—the advantage that it can agree, or refuse, to be identified with the impulses arising in "Myself." This means that it is a conscious being; and to be conscious of Self is to know oneself. Can the "I" know itself?

And if it is I who speak, who are you who listen? Are you your "Myself"? Or are you your "I"?

Where will all this analysis lead me if I continue in this vein? Why, my personality will seem so rich and complex, my brain will be filled with a wealth of new notions and "Myself" will take the glory of it! I could, no doubt, take "Myself" by surprise, if I were to insist on analyzing out my physical mechanism, my emotional impulses, and the unresting whirlpool of my thoughts and imaginations. But what part does the "I" play in all this dissection?

And again, if this "I" were a unit, a consciousness with one unalterable mode of expression, one would expect that all these analyses would in the end reveal its presence.

But it does not take much experiment to convince one that there is a duality in one's guiding impulses: some are pitilessly personal, and seem to intensify the individual's egotism, and some show a spirit of altruism which will sacrifice the Self for a pure ideal. Is there any hope of discovering in oneself a factor of permanent stability, a "managing director" of one's incarnation, aware of its goal and able to enlighten us concerning the route toward it?

This brings us back to the threshold of our original anxiety; but regarding the object of our quest we have made a little progress: we have had a glimpse of the real meaning of consciousness, and of its immanence in all being. Animals are controlled by it, but man, when the automatic life does not satisfy him, wants something more. His legitimate pride, as a candidate for higher realms, seeks instinctively for some element of certainty in himself which could put an end to the duel between his two contradictory tendencies. This, alas, is a hopeless dream in the duality of the natural world. Yet that which is impossible to the "natural" man is possible to one who has awakened in himself the Spiritual Witness.

For although its presence does not exclude that of the Permanent Witness, it is the means of further evolution for the latter, and, where it predominates, the suprahuman state can be attained; and one may then speak of a single consciousness, permanent and immortal, in which the struggle is no longer discord but simply experience seeking through choice an increase of Knowledge.

Until that is attained, we have to admit our duality, and not stifle our anxiety by a cowardly acceptance of our own automatism. After all, the cause of our anxiety is ignorance, and the incoherence of the guidance we can give ourselves. And no theorizing will solve the difficulty.

So, following faithfully the course mapped out, we must eliminate all complexity, fix our attention on the heart of the problem, and rediscover the simplicity of a child.

Let us try for a few moments to establish some sort of mediation between "I," "You," and "the Others." Whoever is speaking or listening, "I" is to be the one who speaks, "You" is to be the one who listens. Let us make no further distinctions, and try to establish a means of mediation.

When a child suckles, the milk is the mediation. Between heaven which gives, and the flower which receives, light is the mediation. The mystery is the assimilation of that which is received and absorbed. But the child does not think of the mystery, it simply sucks, and the flower does not think of the mystery, it simply opens, at whatever time it can receive what it requires.

This is Wisdom—wisdom which knows the necessary gesture to perform the necessary function at the necessary moment.

If there is no opposition or dissociation, then gesture, function, and wisdom are one in giver and receiver.

A child has this innate Knowledge so long as it has not left the Kingdom of Heaven. An infant is not in hope of the Kingdom of Heaven; so long as it has not quitted the state of innocence, which is nondifferentiation, it is in the Kingdom of Heaven. On quitting it, it will painfully have to learn discrimination, what to do and what not to do, in fact the hard task of the man with two wills who cannot distinguish between the voices of the two witnesses when they whisper to him contradictory advice. But later, of course, things will be simpler; the Permanent Witness will be the only one he listens to.

But You and I know this drama, and are tired of submitting blindly. So let us try now to discover consciously the key of the kingdom that we have lost. Let us try to listen, as a child listens, to that vibration in the depths of one's breast which corresponds to the conception of a reality. Let us try, as a child tries, until "it happens." To try is in itself to free oneself from the habit-bound will, and to enlarge the scope of one's intuitive powers.

Listen then, listen unremittingly. Watch the flower open just when it needs the sun. Watch its desire. Watch that in yourself which seeks, in order to discover who the seeker is, and what you seek. Watch the invisible, and slowly your interior vision will open, just as your eyes accustom themselves to see in darkness.

Our principal resistance is fear of being deceived, of escaping from the control of our intellectual faculties. But one can reply to this that sense-perception and false reasoning can also cause delusions. That, however, is part of the world you know, and its verification must be studied elsewhere. For the present we want to set ajar a door into a world which you did not know existed within yourself. It has, sometimes, swung open a little without your knowledge, but that has been more shocking than to open it deliberately.

Knowledge is not to learn and file somewhere in the brain notions which will vanish when the brain cells die. Knowledge is to open one's eyes to the nature of a thing as if one were born into it, so that this perception awakens awareness of that in ourselves which is analogous to it.

If I put myself in a state of complete mental and physical relaxation, if I do not attempt to believe or profess to know, then I can hear in myself the overtones of that which I wish to know, just as a harp sounds all the overtones of the note one touches.

Experience has shown that the doctor who in imagination can identify himself with his patient will prescribe an effective treatment, just as the mountaineer, the explorer, and the lion tamer can avoid the dangers which they have felt approaching and have been experiencing in imagination. But, to reach this condition consciously, one must deliberately abandon the fruitless discussions caused by a variety of doctrines and opinions; one must renounce controversy and quarreling, and march by the single star that hangs over the cradle of the child.

And this is your own star, that of the child which slumbers in you, awaiting its awakening. To discover the straight course which is your own and not another's, you must set out simple in mind, the head and memory empty, and the heart on fire with longing to open yourself unconstrainedly; and the eyes as easily astonished as those of an ignorant child, for whom the world is new.

As a child, you were carried away by thrills of emotion, by delight in the marvelous. You did not dissect the world like a dead body, or

anesthetize your perception in little watertight compartments of material-
ism and spiritualism and monism. You submitted to the charm of legends
and mysteries, and were happy, in being small, to admire powers greater
than yourself. What have you gained by all this suspicious skepticism? Are
you so great that the idea of the suprahuman seems impossible? Or are you
so ashamed of your mediocrity that the notion of suprahumanity offends
you?

Enough of these tergiversations! If you are satisfied with life, ask
nothing more. But if you seek the Light, let us set off together as pilgrims
through the light and shade of mystery.

What is the "mystery"? Have you looked for it in yourself?

Stand before a mirror, and unveil, if you can, the mystery of your
image. Who is that looking at you? Is it yourself? Yourself, looking at
your self? No, it is the reflection, and reflections are an effect of light and
shadow on something which reflects the light projected on it, or rather,
which projects itself by stopping the light.

And what are you yourself? Light? Shadow? Or thing? Of what light
are you the shadow? Of what forces are you the form? Of what are you the
projection?

Observe your reflection, and the contour of your body, which
apparently delimits your life. That, the body, is the thing for which you do
everything; for it you will your daily life, for it you work, for it you love,
for it you fear, and you struggle to preserve its physical life, to satisfy its
senses, tastes, and appetites.

Look at it. Has it ever told you who it is? Or what it will give you for all
your trouble?

Ask it! Try to extort their secret from those eyes which express so little
of the struggle of a soul which is your own! Discover their meaning, if you
can.

"Who are you, my body, you have a little world at your service all
through life? Whence comes thy form, O Form? Answer me! You are
me, you must know me! And me, who am I? Myself, or You? It's
hopeless! If you shut those eyes of mine, I can still see you, within myself;
but you, the reflection, cannot be aware of me. So there is a Myself, which
knows, and a reflection?"

Listen now. In your breast there is something moving. Its impulses
control the flow of your blood, which it receives back and sends out
without rest or pause, and it has been beating since it existed; but it has
been beating without your knowledge. It beats every second of your
existence, but what knowledge of it have you? Try to stop it. You cannot,
your will knows nothing of it. Only your emotion can quicken it.

What! An immaterial impulse act on a physical object? Let the intellect explain that!

Uncontrolled by you, that heart of yours beats out the tempo of your life, and, be it fast or slow, what can you do about it? That is the tempo of your life, your rhythm, your own; everyone has his own.

What cosmic rhythm has regulated this pendulum? Do you not know, O most intelligent man? Who obliged you to be the plaything of this mystery?

Perhaps, then, you can understand how your food becomes transformed into your own substance, yours and not that of an animal? Or how matter, chemically transformed by your digestion, can be finally transmuted into a living personified substance, in fact animated by the same energy as your body?

It is no use to reply in chemical terms, for science must stop here; in the ultimate analysis it can only note that the transmutation occurs, without explaining the last phase of it. Neither can it explain how the minute quantity of nutritious matter which the body does not eliminate is sufficient to maintain it. In a child this is even more striking; so great is the disproportion that its growth evidently cannot be explained except by the reception of some external but nonmaterial substance which encourages the multiplication of cells and blood corpuscles.

This growth is a real mystery, of which the biological explanation is inadequate.

But what is a mystery?

We might say that a mystery is the manifestation of a causal law which cannot be penetrated by our sensory or rational faculties. But this definition does not suggest the feeling of sanctity in a mystery. To understand that there are mysteries in the sacred sense of the word, one must realize that we live in a world of appearances, and that in this world, as in a mirror, the image is a reversed reflection of reality.

The image belongs to the world of form, through which we move with our bodies, thoughts, and senses. Reality is the world of the movements of the Spirit, and we live in that too, but without knowing it.

The art of painting, as taught in China, begins with this axiom: "The movement of life is created by the revolutions of the Spirit. If this principle has not been yours from birth, you cannot hope to learn it."

This may seem harsh, but no more so than St. Paul maintaining that "Christ was once offered to bear the sins of many" (Hebrews 9:28). Or the Gospels: "The Son of Man came to give his life a ransom for many" (Mark 10:45). And further: "This is my blood of the new testament, which is shed for many" (Mark 14:24). And the Christ says: "I pray for them; I pray not for the world" (John 17:9).

And again: ''Unto you it is given to know the mystery of the Kingdom of God: but unto them that are without, all these things are done in parables: that seeing they may see, and not perceive; and hearing they may hear, and not understand; lest at any time they should be converted, and their sins should be forgiven them'' (Mark 4:11-12).

In clearer and more modern language we might say: If the Mystery can only be perceived by the elect, that is to say, by individuals who have had from birth the faculty of perceiving ''the revolutions of the Spirit which create the movement of life,'' how can you expect it to be understood by the crowd, and especially by people who are too intelligent to accept any perception other than from their material senses and their reason?

Must we conclude that the perception of the world of Causes is forever closed to humanity? By merely human means, it is. But all the true initiators have come to earth expressly to indicate the suprahuman means. And whether the World of Causes be called ''Tao'' or ''The Kingdom of Heaven,'' the essential means for attaining it is the same: simplicity of heart and mind.

10

The Discernment of Discernment

The word ''discernment'' will be used here to signify the power to discriminate between a perceived reality and the possibility that the perception may be illusory. Discernment is not the same as faith, for faith may be a personal creation, either mental or emotional, but discernment is a quite certain recognition of the reality or truth of something, and is acquired by the higher consciousness.

Every certainty is the result of an experience. If the experience has come through the senses, the emotions, or the intellect, then the certainty is no more than relative; it is beyond doubt only when it is the fruit of a genuine spiritual experience of identificaton.

Identification is the union of a part of one's being with the object contemplated, whether or not this object is in the field of sensory perception.

True identification is communion between the perceiver and the perceived, and this communion does not permit the intrusion of any notions foreign to the reality of the object contemplated. It demands accordingly the exclusion of all notions or impressions arising from the personality of the perceiver, for these might corrupt the integrity of his perception; that is, it requires absolute neutrality, whether this is obtained accidentally for a moment or by perfect control.

Perfect control of our mental faculties, by holding them steady and reducing them to the role of an absolutely neutral observer, makes identification possible, and conscious identification obtained in these conditions amounts to certain knowledge.*

*No other form of "knowledge" is anything more than inference. (Trans. note)

Identification can also happen accidentally through momentary emptiness of the mind; but in that case it is without the conscious control which coordinates spiritual perceptions, and is thus an unconscious identification. Most intuitive perceptions are of this order and cannot have the value of certainties for lack of the necessary "discernment"; they remain probabilities which must be evaluated more and more closely by a process of verfication strictly purified from personal prejudice.

The possibility of distinguishing without error between the certainty and the mere probability of an experience of identification may be called "the discernment of discernment."

The value of a flash of discernment cannot be measured in time; it is a moment of wisdom, of true knowledge. A sage may enjoy such moments more or less frequently, but they are never continuous so long as he is obliged to undergo the accidents and relativism of life on earth.

The discernment of a true discernment requires in the man who would practice it an experimental knowledge of his own different states of consciousness and of the value of the evidence they offer him. Only in such a case can our discernment have the value of reality, and thus allow us to find our answers in ourselves.

11

The Milieu

For the genesis of anything, the first necessity is the formation of a proper milieu.

This is brought about by spiritual influence. For if you have not in yourself the Will to the Light, you are like a magnet which has lost its magnetism, or a bird which has lost its wings, unable to move and obliged to submit passively to the laws of its environment.

If you desire liberation, you must become your own "milieu" and bring forth your own Light, completing your cycle in yourself.

But this cycle must genuinely correspond to your original destiny. If you wish to bring forth the divine Light of Wisdom, do not provide for it the unstable milieu of your maladjusted personality. And beware what powers you attract by your desires and prayers!

How few are those who can draw down the divine Power directly and simply, without formulas and names, "in Spirit and in Truth." They are the true "poor in spirit," who desire "in Truth," and theirs in the only desire that deserves to be so called, for it yearns only for That, lives for That, unites itself to That, just as a flower drinks its life from the light; for this Desire is in them a vital necessity, and the necessity is that of their own divine spark demanding its sustenance.

For such, the Kingdom of Heaven is indeed within them because they are in it; for that which is not separated is one, and this Desire is nonseparation.

The obstructions to this Desire are all those things that men call desires. The desires of the earthly are attached to all that is not That, because That—the Spirit— seems to them the Void; and men fear the Void. So, to escape it, they listen to all their desires, and these desires are not the

Desire, but either wishes (which are mental) or else affinities created by the need for finding one's complement. Thus is Nature's work continued; and this is the Kingdom of Earth.

Many are those who project their imaginings outside themselves and create gods "in their own image and likeness." The powers they would adore are those that can grant them all the boons they yearn for in this world and the next. They are answered by Christ's word: "Ye know not what ye ask" (Mark 10:38).

Their wish is for an idol to protect and favor them, or else for a divine being who can be loved possessively. But paradises, like gods, are made by men according to their desires, and their misfortune will be that they will often find what they have imagined. But what we can imagine is no part of the inexpressible Divine.

An omnipotent desire is one which animates the very cells of your being and makes you able to seize and grasp the object of your affinity. Such a desire has magic power, and, like the sorcerer's apprentice, man uses it imprudently. For the god, or power, which answers him is of the same nature as his desire. The money-grubber invokes the powers of money, the social climber the powers of the social order, and the thinker invokes intellectual powers. Thus the seeker is ruled and restricted by his affinity. This is his hell, or purgatory, in which he is already confined in this present life.

As for so-called "spiritual desires," the potency of "the Desire" must not be confused with these anemic wishes for spirituality, or emotional longings toward some God or other who is expected to reciprocate, to show good intentions, and to provide all the scenic effects which lull the pious into an illusion of beatitude.

What do I gain if I deceive myself? Only my mortal being can be deceived. When the illusory vanishes, reality appears. The necessary experience is to recognize the real in the midst of the world of illusion.

To do this I must clear my own ground, eliminate all that is not my true self, and create in myself the milieu which can attract the Spirit. Only the immortal Self can eliminate personal desires and so serve the one true Desire, Desire for the Eternal. And then the Permanent Witness will submit without reserve to the supremacy of the Spiritual Witness.

Environment

The Milieu is that wherein the complementary opposites meet are adjusted together.

The Means is that which brings them together.

And this Means, this possibility of concord, is the knowledge of how to create a harmonious milieu.

Environment

Every milieu that is pure, and ripe to receive seed, will easily bear the fruit of its own king.

Purity, however, does not consist in the absence of dirt, physical or moral, as the world erroneously thinks. The purity of a thing is its homogeneousness, in accordance with its own particular type. A man is perfectly pure at whatever moment he is totally identified with the cosmic character of his Being. A scorpion too can be perfectly pure, and is so, insofar as it is perfectly true to its nature. Any concession that weakens the essential rhythm of a being puts it into a heterogeneous and therefore impure condition. For, as Hippocrates said, ''the homogeneous will join with the homogeneous, but the heterogeneous fights, resists, and separates.'' Thus any mixture of blood, or of divergent tendencies, creates a battlefield. And equally, the forced creation of a milieu for some arbitrary ideal, or for qualities foreign to its nature, can only give birth to monsters and be a source of needless strife.

If the fruit is to be sound, the milieu must be in harmony with the nature of the seed.

Thus, for the creation of such a milieu in oneself, the first requisite is a knowledge of all the deepest tendencies of one's real being.

The second condition is to awaken and reeducate the inner perceptions.

The third is to cultivate and intensify the Will to the Light.

SEEKING OUT TENDENCIES

If in the revealing light of some moment of cataclysm you were to meet your double, not dressed in its worldly glad-rags, not armed with that buckler of excuses which conventional hypocrisy uses to cover our secret wishes, but in all its moral nakedness, showing its tendencies and urges, its pitiless cunning and its cowardice, are you certain that you would recognize it?

How many sages are there on this earth who could and calmly would call by their real names the secret motives of their actions?

That, nevertheless, would be the greatest victory a man could gain over himself, and the first proof of his mastery—a clear vision of all the tendencies which rule his inner being.

If you want to enjoy the sympathy of the crowd, if you want normal people to make excuses for you, do not enter the maze to which this fearless search will lead you. Remain in the disguising shade, where reassuring mediocrity comes down and veils any truth that should threaten to show its face and, to discourage inquiries, covers it with a well-known label. For quite possibly the unveiling of your secret world might ruffle your calm acceptance of the opinions, values, and prejudices which rule your ordinary life.

But if your aim is to attain Masterhood and Knowledge, then illuminate one day of your life with the cold light of impersonal judgment; observe the finer points of all your impulses, excavate without pity and without excuses, until you lay bare their roots and origins.

You will be surprised, at times, to recognize the signature of your ancestors in certain atavistic ways of behavior, learned or inherited from your family. Other impulses, to which you have given moral value without examining their right to it, will be shown up as mere habitual reflexes of mind or emotion, impressed upon you either by education or by the daily suggestion of your religious and social circumstances.

Both these classes of impulse are foreign to you, and prevent your true nature from manifesting itself.

A third class is your own; observe it therefore, but do not judge it! It consists of passionate impulses, marks of your deepest nature, which can reveal to you by their analogies with the same forces in Nature (in planets, animals, plants, and metals) the characteristics of your true Being, and help you to identify yourself with it.

Let us make a beginning together on this introspection.

The atavistic tendencies which are the signature of a family or a race are the rhythm or type imprinted by contagion, and as it were by a sort of imitation, on all the cells of the body and all the corpuscles of the blood; and the blood, as vehicle of this animal soul, transfuses its characteristics and superficial tendencies from generation to generation until they are effaced by new impressions. This effect will be the deeper, the narrower is the circle in which the family or race is living.

The conformations of family character, though they may be brought out or hidden by relationships with the world outside, have been ingrained by successive generations and cannot be removed except by length of time or violent rupture. Emigrants, transplanted into a race and traditions radically different from their own, often show greater flexibility of habit and judgment, and are often readier for the acceptance of new ideas.

One who looks indulgently on the violent temper he has inherited, or smiles to recognize in his mirror some gesture familiar in his grandfather or father, should rather try to break these chains of servitude, and give attention to the grand object of his journey.

For the great mass of humans, family, country, and religious denomination are an indispensable refuge. But for those who desire to take the narrow way and attain the highest of human possibilities, the Gospel has shown the unconditional requirement: "If any man hate not his father and mother and wife and children, he cannot be my disciple" (Luke 14:26).

The word "hate" does not mean, in the Gospel of Love, that fury which poisons modern society, but rather the exclusiveness which gives precedence to the conquest of Reality, over against all other social duties and relationships.

Here again the choice should be made wholeheartedly. If you are still attached to the fetters of memory, if you are still controlled by the instinct for continuation on earth, then you had better submissively accept the duties of your chosen world, support its customs and traditions even to excess, and observe them so intensely and so consciously that, by contrast, your "sense of eternity" will be awakened and will summon you to the more sacred duty of the individual quest.

But if this longing for Reality predominates already in you, then follow the commandments of liberaton; let go of all that the past has written in your substance: seek your true Name; set yourself apart from the group-soul of any group; and learn that you can serve your fellow-travelers more effectively by becoming, yourself, a sun that shines with its own light rather than by helping them to drag the old chains of slavery.

The same applies to the tendencies engraved upon your cells by the education you were obliged to undergo. Since your life began, all your intellectual reflexes, all your manner of judging things, and of expressing your feelings, were carved and molded by the wills of others, and inhibited the development of your individual consciousness. Now you can free it from this dead weight, knock down the wall of prohibitions and prejudices which prevented you from making your own discoveries.

What do you know of Good and Evil?

Their relative value varies from one race or climate to another; and their absolute value you can only learn by identifying yourself with the Source of all things.

But in order to do this you must let go of all preconceived opinions, all judgments dictated by convenience, all the conventions necessary to social life.

Many so-called sins will hardly weigh as such in the cosmic balance; but many acts ostensibly innocent will lay upon you a heavy burden of karma.

Granted that you incur a debt toward anyone whom you injure by the refusal to discharge an acknowledged duty; granted that you are responsible when you break the laws of the social order; granted too that you have duties to your family, but only to the extent that you have freely accepted them—and for this reason the obligations of marriage and parenthood are more binding than those of filial or fraternal duties.

But a duty in the general interest will always be more important than others, and the first of all these is the duty to make spiritual growth; for one wise action by a man of insight can do more for humanity than a whole life of conventional virtue.

Whoever gives his free consent to being a member of a group is bound thereby to accept its earthly rules and sanctions. But no group, not even a religious group, can have a right to thwart the evolution of an individual either by overruling his conscience or by professing to substitute for the judgment of his own true Destiny its own allegedly "eternal" condemnation, or by granting a pardon which in the absence of true contrition is ineffective.

For the attainment of the suprahuman realm there are certain inexorable requirements, and there can be no excuses, no sentimental concessions to the relative values of the merely human world. For, as the Christ said: "I pray not for the world" (John 17:9).

Thus duty can take strange forms when its motive is the sublime quest for the Light—for example, the obligation on certain Chinese dynasties to destroy the works of their predecessors in order to rebuild in a new spirit. So too certain revolutionary schools of art, and the destructive tendencies of such notions as "permanent revolution," ill-expressed today by social theories based on perverted intuitions. All these bear witness to that urge we have to destroy impermanent values and in the shock of the void to discover the true Light.

It is of course unwise to trust the unawakened with means of destruction which only the sage should wield. Yet no one of the elect will find his "kingdom" except by the pitiless destruction of everything which is not a part of the indestructible life of his own being. And this can only be the Consciousness developed in him by the experience of life.

Blind obedience is for the herd, and mediocrity is its refuge. A boldness that accepts its responsibility is the virtue of the conqueror who would find the keys of his kingdom.

Happy is he who dares to destroy the phantoms of his past in order to find his own eternal likeness. Thrice happy he who is in love with the void, who fears not to plunge into the abyss where creative Faith can lose nothing but its shadow, and the Living Soul nothing but its dead ghost.

You who do not wish to die with your body, cut out and cast in the fire, from among your habits and ideas, all that can be destroyed. The indestructible will reveal itself of itself.

Your deep, your passionate tendencies, are tyrannical forces linked to your destiny just as the need to sing is linked to the throat of a nightingale.

Your needs are elementary forces born of the necessity for a physical organ to discharge its function.

The stomach lives to eat, and to do this it forms juices which attack its food; but if food fails, these acids attack its own substance, and it creates a feeling of pain, which is a cry for help. The pain becomes a sensation of tyrannical necessity, and obliges the animal to kill in order to satisfy it.

From bacteria (the most primitive form of stomach) up to the human animal, this urge expresses itself more and more perfectly; but whether it teaches ambush to the spider, cunning to the fox, or violence to the carnivore, it is still the same obedience to an elementary need.

In an organic being each vital function is the expression of a corresponding need; but the different needs express themselves with different rhythms, in a subtle or gross manner, according to the stage of evolution of the individual and the species. In the lion voracity is held back for a few moments by pride of conquest, and in the cat by its love of play. Where delicacy of perception goes hand in hand with the development of consciousness, its modes of expression can be distinguished by the seven qualities which are the signatures of the seven planets; and these seven modes are themselves derived from combinations of the four fundamental qualities, Hot, Cold, Moist, and Dry.

The ''humors'' of the animal body (blood, lymph, bile, and atrabile) are the materialization of these qualities, and their proportion determines the physical temperament of each individual; that is, it controls the expression of his instincts, and influences his psychological reactions: The bilious type is choleric; the lymphatic, lazy; the sanguine, eager; and the atrabilious, anxious. But these temperaments only modify, by their color and intensity, the passions proper to all animal life.

Obviously, therefore, passional tendencies, being elementary forces of Nature, cannot be suppressed by an act of will. Even the most skillful engineer cannot prevent an underground stream from flowing; he can seal up the spring, but this will only divert its course, and it will reach the surface again through the first fissure that it finds.

Passion must be classed with the instincts, but Consciousness can make use of it as an instrument in the struggle toward the Light.

12

The Visit to the Cave

There was a man who had all that learning, love, and wealth can give, and yet a gnawing anxiety troubled his unsatisfied heart.

He sought relief in travel, but seemed only to be making circles around his anxiety, and every stage led back to his unhappy starting point.

He climbed mountain peaks, but found only danger in them and no escape. He cried, as he crossed the snowy wastes and found them void of life: "Where is the Spirit?"

He crossed the seas, and watched the ocean spend itself on the shore, but nothing revealed to him the mystery of its flowing.

The starry heaven of the Chaldean Magi threw him into a paroxysm of despairing calculations.

The sands of the desert aggravated his fever, for he had not understood their voice and could not bear their silence.

At length he returned to his own country, as unsatisfied as he had set out.

One spring night he was wandering aimlessly in an old oak wood, and as he stood, weary of everything, dreaming beside a broken tree trunk, he remembered a deep cave where dwelt a wise old hermit.

He found it, all gray with smoke, and entering, saw an old man who bade him sit down in front of a fire of dry wood.

He said to the old man: "I have been all over the world, but I have not found 'the answer.'"

"What are you seeking?"

"Truth."

"Can you not read?"

"I have studied all the philosophies."

"What have books to do with Truth?"

"What else is there to read?"

"Are you blind?" asked the hermit. "If you cannot read the truth which is Nature's signature in heaven and earth and in your body, how can you expect to discover her secrets in the writings of men?"

"What is Truth?" said the man.

"That which is."

"How can a man know that?"

"By knowing Nature and himself."

"I know myself very well."

"What do you know of yourself?"

"I know my vices and virtues, my likes and dislikes, my will."

"Is all that yourself? You mistake the crowd for the individual."

"Then who am I?"

"No one can tell you, except your own conscience. When you explored the outside of the earth, you found nothing. Try exploring the inside of your world. You will be surprised."

"I do not know how. Will you guide me?"

"All I can do," replied the sage, "is to blow away the clouds, and that only if you will it in very truth."

The hermit came and sat opposite the seeker. After a silence he said: "Reflect yourself."

The man gazed into the hermit's eyes and observed his image.

He said to the sage: "I see the Other. He is examining your thoughts intently, drawing up a list of clever questions to discover your secrets.... No, that is not I! That is not what I want."

"How do you know? Still, never mind, continue looking. What is he doing now?"

"Magic formulas! He is invoking power, he wants to control men, to compel love, he is forging his will like steel to avenge an injury. It is terrible, he wants to...."

"Let him! His will will come back on his own head."

"Stop him!" cried the man. "He will go mad!"

"I cannot. Only you can renounce these accursed 'powers.' Do you truly want to?"

"I renounce them."

The hermit effaced the vision with a gesture.

"If I can efface it," he said, "that means it is not yourself. Now search in yourself." And he placed his fingers on the man's temples.

"Here is myself...my thoughts."

"Indeed?" The hermit smiled.

The man pondered for a moment, his eyes closed.

"No," he concluded, "I was wrong, they are just a crowd, a mad fandango of confused ideas, one following another wildly. When one melts away others come along, one suggests another, they get transposed, multiplied, divided. I cannot follow it, it is a mad rush!''

Irritated, the seeker became involved in the game; he saw himself face to face with confusion and trying vainly to stop its course. Ideas came and went in every direction, beliefs struggled together, doubts tugged at him, every sort of opinion charged at him, all trying to overwhelm him. He struggled, tried to fight a way through, pushed them away in the hope of casting a look behind, but others still rushed in.

''Stop!'' he cried. ''This is sheer confusion!''

The hermit made a gesture, and the movements became slower, and as in a slow-motion film details were seen which before had passed unnoticed. The intricate complications became clearer, and revealed the chain of their causation.

The seeker was astounded. All his intelligent ideas seemed to go strangely lame. What he had called ''logical'' was suddenly demolished by an unforeseen consequence. He saw what knotted strings led up to an act he had thought spontaneous. He could follow his thoughts right back to their origins, and was astonished at their diversity. What? All these inspirations, which he had thought his own, came to him from without?

His professional achievement showed as a compact group of extraneous notions. His most superb idea had come from a rival! Others, in long entwining chains, had come from his family tradition. But most had been snatched in passing from a thousand other influences, and arduously worked in with oddments of reading and his personal studies. How could he claim to be the father of all that?

''How long will this horrible dance continue?'' he exclaimed.

''Until death of your brain.''

''What will remain after that?''

''Vague floating forms such as you see, without aim or order.''

''What will become of those forms?''

''They will become the property of other brains, which they will touch unnoticed.''

''But what shall I get out of it all?''

''Nothing, because your instrument will no longer exist.''

''I am not missing much, am I?'' he sighed. ''So little of that was myself! But then where is my Self?''

''You must continue the search.''

The hermit touched the man's solar plexus. He shivered, and waves of emotion swept over him like a rising tide. Hope, love, and malice flowed over him, just as he had known them not long since, and he trembled.

''I know all these,'' he cried. ''Why do you bring them back?''

But eagerly he lived them over again, trying in vain to catch the ideas he loved and push away the sufferings which were too intense. Wearily he tried to expunge them, but they only changed, and were replaced by older ones; like a film shown backward, memories flooded up, reversing the course of time. He watched them uncomprehending. At the passionate adventures in which his reflection was involved he now felt no emotion; quite undisturbed he watched it sinking into despair or rising to paroxysms of joy; at the most, an indulgent smile for one or two excesses. He was amazed at the waves of bliss which had filled certain scenes, and rejected the storms of anger which no longer seemed to have any meaning.

And where was he himself, the Self of today, in this long story about the past? That in him which could still respond to those echoes had now such different vibrations! Were there, in all these waves of movement, just a few which composed his own true harmony? If so, how could he recognize them?

The hermit, answering his secret thought, said: "To know that, you must explore even deeper." And he placed his hand on the back of the seeker's neck.

For a moment the man was silent, then a violent shudder went through him, and the blood reddened his face.

Revolted, he exclaimed: "What have I to do with these horrors? I have rejected all these obsessions! They do not concern me!"

"If you have been liberated from them, why do they trouble you?"

The man trembled, trying in vain to escape from what had been evoked; but gradually and in spite of himself, panting and sweating, he succumbed to its grip. Burning images flowed over him, sensual folly played with temptations and tortuous perversions, while possessive rage confounded vivid eroticism with surly sadism. This was the witches' sabbath of his dreams.

The hermit let the storm die down, and the man asked brokenly: "I came in search of peace. Why have you aroused my demons?"

"You came in search of Truth. Peace is its fruit. We must first reactivate your deepest roots."

"Are they buried in that crowd?"

"Vice comes from a deviation of the natural tendencies of your being. It works out as opposition to your true destiny."

"Must one allow these oppositions to grow strong?"

"It is indispensable for the enlargement of consciousness that you recognize them as such."

"Is consciousness found in the dunghill?" the man asked with a sour smile.

"That is truer than you think! Contradictory forces show their true nature when they come into conflict. The specific quality incarnated in you will be revealed by the shock of contrast. For instance, the Martian nature, made all of violence, will easily be enslaved by Venus. The Venusian, seeking for beauty, will rather plunge himself in filth in order to heighten his awareness of beauty. The Solar type, which is dominating, can be a masochist. And the Saturnian, who loves solitude and mystery, often looks for his complement in exhibitionism.''

''Can the Spirit not be reborn in man without these troubles?''

''Before the resurrection comes the descent into hell.''

''Where is hell? Do you know?''

''In the bowels of the earth of your body! But its fire is also that which causes the resurrection!''

''How can the same principle bring forth opposite effects?''

''When your soul was incarnated in matter, it married itself to the baseness of matter; it can only free itself by subtilizing that which has become bound to it by attraction.''

''That does not answer my question.''

''Because you fail to see the double movement of life. Separation resulted from the need to see oneself reflected; attraction is the result of the need for reunification. But reunification cannot happen until each complement has become perfectly itself. And how could it do that except by recognizing all its tendencies?''

''So regeneration is only possible by diving into all this filth?''

''I did not say that! No sage would advise a man to put into practice all the filthiness he finds in himself. But no attainment is possible if you shut out the light for fear of thieves and fire. The only way—and you must face it—is to let all your impressions rise to the surface, with all your impulses and urges, and there observe them without telling yourself lies about them, and so learn to play on their contrasts in order to arouse your consciousness of their cosmic tendency, which is their mainspring.''

The man pondered, and asked: ''Playing with fire, isn't it?''

''Is fire any safer hidden beneath its ash? Surely you are not any longer the victim of these obsessions?''

''No...unless perhaps in dreams.''

''Your dreams are the mirror of your reality. When you escape in sleep from the prison of your intellect, then your instincts show themselves in their true colors, and prove that the force you thought extinguished was merely held in check.''

The seeker remarked angrily: ''So little good have I seen as I went about the world, and so much ill, that I have condemned any sin which offended my dignity!''

The hermit smiled. ''You will be judged by that which you judge, and condemned by that which you condemn.''

''I do not understand.''

''That, for oneself, is sin, which one judges to be a sin. Thus, without knowing it, you make your own law, at your own risk and peril.''

''But that is perfectly amoral! Much better refuse to recognize Evil at all!''

''Your conclusion is unsound. The aim, remember, is to attain knowledge of the essential principal behind Good and Evil, and then to understand how it relates to the experience of every individual.''

''What is the Law then?''

''Learn to know yourself, to the depth of your profoundest instincts. Just as a lion tamer tries an animal until he knows its every trick, so must you outface your most hidden reflexes, and then do whatever your newly developed consciousness will let you do.''

''That law sounds too flexible, and too arbitrary.''

''It is more rigid than you can possibly imagine. Perception of danger is the best of guides.''

''And if I fall by the way?''

''I did not advise you to put into practice all your instincts, only to uncover and recognize them. What more could you have to fear than you have now? Today your soul is a jungle, much of it unexplored. You must throw light into all its dark corners, search out all its dangerous beasts and reptiles, that heterogeneous collection that you still conceal behind the little word ''I.'' Learn to recognize them by their appetites, to become aware of their tricks. Some will be strange to you; others are a part of your kingdom. When they are all docile to your orders, you will know in what your true Self consists.

''When you have learned that, return to me. When the corn is ripe, and the grapes are beginning to color, then if I find you so disposed I will try to widen your horizon.''

13

The Sexual Problem

Sex presents a problem which cannot be evaded if one wishes to use its power for development toward the suprahuman; but the mere satisfaction of instinct retards development.

Certain doctrines preach the use of sexual excitement as a means of awakening higher faculties and extraordinary powers, but such methods are really dangerous and should be shunned. What they evoke is not the higher faculties, but unhealthy forces from which it is then almost impossible to free oneself. This is one of the greatest perils a man can be involved in, for he becomes the slave of these powers, and runs the risk of complete nervous and mental unbalance.

On the other hand, the repression of the sexual instinct is equally a danger. Psychology has demonstrated that a passion violently thwarted is stifled rather than overcome. Conquest is only real when the adversary is disarmed by a more powerful expression of the vital force.

So long as we exist in physical bodies, we are subject to Nature's law of dualization, by which affinity is created between complementary opposites which are separated. This dualization, which is the foundation of Nature and its basic evil, is also the foundation of terrestrial experience, the object of which is to transcend Nature and return to union with the One. It is also the foundation of our cultivation of consciousness, since it gives us the possibility of choice between opposite qualities, between the real and the relative, between what is good or evil for us at the moment.

This dualization, being the cause of affinity between complementary opposites, is the cause of sexuality and of the desire that men call love. The error is to confuse love, desire, and need.

Need is an appetite, and only concerns the physical body. Needs are therefore of the animal nature, the result of physiological functions stimulated at the appropriate point of the natural cycle.

Desire, when aroused by need or instinct, is a purely animal impulse. But, quite apart from animal impulses, desire can exist in man as an affinity for qualities or states of being of a more subtle sort. As a rule, however, we are not conscious of its deeper cause, and so we pervert the character of such a desire by confusing it with mere wishes, or even needs, and use it as an excuse for gratifying them, and thus the idea of love is vulgarized.

Yet the idea of love, although applied to sexual desire, is a symbol of the absolute Love which has no single object, and which is the fruit of awareness of mutual solidarity.

Sexual selection by affinity is a present manifestation of this cosmic love. The danger lies in confusing the origins of the various emotions of love—physical, sentimental, ''ideal,'' or even supposedly spiritual—for they have generally a sexual foundation, whether conscious or unconscious.

For the relation of sex to the brain and liver is either forgotten or unknown. These three factors, the grand triad of the Personality, affect one another so closely that it is often difficult to distinguish which of them is responsible for a sudden stirring of passion, desire, or thought. If one of them is overexcited or in abeyance, the other two are affected, and produce feelings which the man, unaware of the interaction, takes seriously, not suspecting their physioloical origin.

Besides the sexual stirrings produced by the cycles of Nature and human life, each individual is influenced by his own particular instincts, which make him react sexually to certain actions or circumstances.

These instinctive characteristics are recorded in the liver, but produce reactions in the sex glands and the brain, and these two, being always in alliance, offer each other excuses for explaining and satisfying the resulting longings.

The unawakened man is overtaken by these impulses and easily becomes their slave, spending his energy on them but not becoming enlightened. But he who wishes to escape from his animal nature will sincerely try to uncover his instincts and observe their working. He will of course lose the exciting effect of being taken by surprise, but he will gain in exchange the opportunity of using his instincts consciously to increase his ''vital fire,'' instead of prostituting the idea of love by confusing it with the satisfaction of an instinct.

Sexual energy has the same origin as the subtle fire which gives life. It is for man to use it wisely or else expend it thoughtlessly.

He whose aim is satisfaction will refuse to learn control, preferring to be at the mercy of surprises and receive his pleasure without effort. But the man who has in him, even unconsciously, a sense of the true Love, will be ashamed of animal sexuality, except in the service of perpetuating the species. This comes from his moral sense, the voice of conscience, which is our judge.

Then the problem arises, what to do with the vital fire? Should one suffocate it, or can it be used to raise us to a higher life?

To deny or suffocate sexual excitement is an act of suppression dictated by the will, and results only too often in redirecting the energy into intellectual or sentimental imaginings, with psychological trouble as a frequent consequence. Alternatively, continual suppression may lead to flaccidity, which is the way of death and not of life; for impotence is not the same as mastery!

True mastery, without unfortunate consequences, is only attained when an inferior joy is replaced by a higher one.

If slavery to sensual pleasure is an animal slavery, on the other hand conscious desire is of the human realm; indeed it is the key to life and liberation, once it is clarified, that is, stripped of artificial excuses.

That desire, which is the key of life, seeks to increase the vital fire, and can be stirred or exalted either by sexual excitement or by the Will to the Light.

Sexual excitement makes desire hypocritical if it has to excuse itself with aestheticism, sentimentality, and intellectual erotic imaginations. For all forms of eroticism are basically the search for emotional shock. And the cause of this emotional shock is an act which suddenly upsets the balance of our feelings; it violates our normal standard of feelings about morality, or about love and friendship, about reputation or security.

Whether the shock is given by pain or joy or anguish, it is always a loss of balance which upsets our natural inertia. The shock is desired for excitement's sake; and if the aim of the excitement is sexual satisfaction, nothing will be gained but the one sensual pleasure. A more conscious being, who looks for a higher joy, will desire the shock in order to strengthen his interior fire.

In any case, therefore, to desire an emotional shock is to desire a loss of equilibrium. Any excess can do this, but erotic excess does it to increase the heat of sexual feeling.

Erotic perversions are always a compensation for the tyranny of the Ego. Masochism is inverted authoritarianism, and the wallowing in degradation is the inversion, or mortification, of sensual aestheticism.

If their aim is only animal pleasure and satisfaction, erotic impulses can debase; but equally, if the intention is the opposite, they can serve like other emotional shocks to enhance consciousness and life.

The difference lies in the aim and in the mode of application.

A man who risks his life for an impersonal cause may find an exaltation in the fear of danger because of the joy of sacrificing his purely selfish security.

If you can choose at will either to yield deliberately to your animal nature, without making excuses for it, or else to control it and find in doing so the exaltation of sacrifice, then you have found one of the keys of life, the key to the transmutation of the vital fire.

The joy of overcoming oneself transforms the desire for a fugitive pleasure into desire for the infinite Joy. This cannot be too often repeated.

14

The Pendulum

Spirit is the substantial source of "things"; but "things" become opposed to Spirit; "things" are passive and react.

Man, in his Automatic Self, is a "thing"; he does not discern the source of his impulses, but submits to them passively like a reed in the wind; he is their plaything when unaware of them, and if he revolts against them he must suffer from their resistance.

Thus by the law of alternation he swings to and fro like a pendulum: effort—impotence; hope—despair.

And the law of reaction means that the higher the rise, the more grievous the fall. Instead of this one can learn to "live" the pendulum; and therein can Wisdom be found.

For the alternation is inevitable. To recognize it is to abolish the anxiety that comes of ignorance; to have its measure is to be able to master it; not to resist it is to attain peace; and to use its impetus is to increase one's vital force.

The movement has four phases:

First phase: Will to power and mastery

Second phase: Lack of balance

Third phase: Absence of will

Fourth phase: Balanced serenity.

The will to power gives the impetus to mount, and pitiful indeed is the timid man who does not dare to use it. False humility keeps his soul enslaved, taking a morbid satisfaction in his wretchedness. This is the putrid virtue of mediocrity.

The aim of every tradition of wisdom is to gain possession of the "inner kingdom," for to hold that is the key to the "Kingdom of Heaven," which is a kingdom not of this earth. But the man who seeks it has his feet on the ground, and his body is his instrument. His personal form is the obstacle he must overcome, but the Will to the Light reveals from time to time the Secret Being within him.

The true Name of that Being, though unknown to its bearer, is the thread that binds together all his existences, and its consciousness is the "divine kingdom" in which the human Personality becomes the servant of its Immortal Self.

This victory of the suprahuman, being the highest aim we can have on earth, is not won without striking a blow; and the Lower Self is both the weapon to be used and the intended victim. Its resistance therefore is inevitable, and its instinct of self-preservation classes the Individuality as its opponent.

But the prospect of power will draw it like a bait.

The power is perfectly real. Mastery of the physical body gives health and strength; mastery of the emotions prevents one from being controlled by others, and opens the inward ear; mastery of the mind, by which the arising thoughts can be either formulated or abolished at will, makes possible intuitive vision.

The prospect of such power as this should surely suffice to overcome inertia. And we shall be wise to use it, for it will give us the impetus to mount. Only we must remain alert to substitute the Will to the Light for the will to power; for thus at every upward step the quality of the power will be less personal and more altruistic, since it comes from mastery over the grasping instinct of our egocentric nature.

The aim of the whole operation is to give the pendulum energy.

The moment of success is critical, for the notion of reaching the limit restricts effort and leads to a falling back. This is where wisdom should intervene; for, realizing the instability of the success obtained, it would accept the limit as the prerequisite of a new creative impulse—which will arise, but not before its proper time. That is the secret!

Worldly persons dislike this game intensely, for if they make an effort they expect to enjoy the fruits of it; so to prevent the falling back they use their willpower to insist upon a result—and the pendulum breaks.

The third phase of the pendulum is, mystically speaking, the compensation for the proud effort of power, namely absence of will, which means acceptance, not of impotence but of the vital law of alternation. It accepts the phase of descent without resistance, being certain that a new phase of energy will follow. And in a similar way our understanding of the pendulum's action can be enlarged from the merely personal field to the universal.

The decisive moment is when the pendulum's further movement is rejected by the proud man who refuses to accept descent, and justified in him who does accept it.

For the humility of the sage is to understand that power is only knowledge of the law.

He who accepts the descent will find at the bottom of it the fruit of his awareness of it, namely serenity and balance.

Thus is that peace attained which gives renewed impetus for a further rise by means of a legitimate will to power.

The amplitude of the pendulum's swing is determined by one's own stage of awareness; but without a fresh impulse it tends to diminish. This is the justification of the means suggested to set it going, namely the arousing of a personal instinct in order to start the game which in the end will destroy the personal attitude by forcing it to acknowledge the law of alternation.

Absolute cessation of alternation could only be the result of universalization of consciousness.

This path, which makes use of the contradictions in an individual's nature, is the contrary of that which tries to abolish weaknesses by denying their existence; that only creates inhibitions.

The pendular movement is continually exemplifed in the alternation of dilation and contraction, and we should learn to make use of it.

The air penetrates our bodies by the double movement of respiration; and, like our lungs, the earth itself expands and contracts.

All things living on earth partake of this alternation between dilation and contraction, inspiration and expiration.

Dilation is the happy moment of expanding into oneness.

Contraction is the satanic function of materialization.

Both are necessary, but to use them wisely one must understand their motive forces.

Dilation is a gesture of union, of absorption into the Cosmos, without selection, opposition, or separation. Its tendency is to expansion, to the breaking of bounds, to the fusion of all in All. It is the absence of personal will, the opening of the heart without reserve, the attempt to escape into the Abyss beyond the frontiers of matter. It is the upward movement of the pendulum; but the pendulum falls inevitably back, since its point of attachment is on earth.

Its descent is the movement of expiration and contraction.

All things except the Absolute Unity are subject to this alternation; it is the most inexorable motion in the becoming of the universe.

For this reason Wisdom does not seek peace in continual "Good," without ugliness and without a falling back, but rather in the skillful use of oppositions.

Dilation is inevitably followed by contraction, and therefore all progress, all generous expansion is at once followed by a reaction. If you wish to know what the reaction will be, consider your private motives for resistance, for it will take their character; and they will be your intellectual criticisms, your doubts and rebellions, your skepticism and pessimism.

If you are not aware of this reaction, it will control you, and you may sadly conclude that the progress which you made in the period of expansion has been all wiped out in the period of contraction. Thus do men of goodwill, if they are ignorant victims of this lamentable seesaw, proceed with their spiritual evolution at the speed of a tortoise.

To attain victory quickly, one must become aware of the contrary rhythm and learn to take advantage of its movement in the antagonistic direction, just as a blacksmith uses the rebound of his hammer to diminish its deadweight; the anvil, by its resistance, throws up the hammer, and the blacksmith requires less effort to bring it down again.

The rebound increases with repetition up to a certain number of strokes, determined by the fatigue of the metal, which also needs its intervals of rest.

Consider this law carefully, and draw the conclusion.

The phase of contraction is a necessary evil; how can you make use of it?

Every action increases in amplitude if encouraged by a reaction.

Contraction is a satanic tautening of muscle in order to hold what one has grasped; it is the avarice of Matter storing up its nourishment in itself.

It is the fear of losing oneself, the turning in upon oneself, the need to know one's limits in order to lock up the ego in an impenetrable shell.

Contraction condenses and concretizes. When you feel it coming over you, bring your progress down to the material level; act, execute, write down what you have learned in the period of exaltation. This is the exact opposite of what the Automaton does; he submits to the phase of depression as a phase of impotence, and lets gloom and resentment torture him in vain.

The expansive phase, on the other hand, the Automaton uses up in exuberant action, distracting and dispersing himself, in fact wasting and scattering the vitality that he receives in that phase.

One should observe this ebb and flow attentively, and use the pendular rhythm to increase one's strength. In the period of expansion one should seek silence, lengthen one's meditations, and stay quiet as much as possible in order to listen, to heat up the inner fire. You waste your treasure if you yield to the temptation of externalizing your joy in talk and action. Your ardor should expand not outwardly but inwardly. For only calm and silence can give full power to the phases of impulse, expansion, and self-giving, which will revitalize your being.

Exterior action should be reserved for the dark period of contraction. In this phase of harshness and cold assert your conquests, materialize your dreams, and bring to concrete expression that which you understood and assimilated in the phase of joy. Like the blacksmith, use reaction to assist action, to give form to what you have conceived.

The astringent side of one's nature can be used to give clarity and form to new knowledge.

And if the combative mood prevails in spite of everything, set it an absorbing intellectual or manual task; this is much better than to let it impede your progress.

15

Watchfulness and Mediation

When the Automatic Self and its brain-consciousness have been brought under conscious control, then we have reached the stage at which power belongs to the Permanent Witness. The alliance of the two creates an awakened being who is free to make use of his physical, emotional, and mental equipment. But to reach even this stage of mastery requires unremitting disciplined effort.

Our earlier descriptions of the constitution of man and the coordination of his organic functions were only explanations of what one needs to know in order to treat functional disorders and deficiencies. But to know is not of itself to understand, and self-knowledge requires a keen awareness of all our constituent elements, mental, emotional, and physical. These are the three aspects of the automatic "I," and there is the greatest difficulty in deciding which is the prime mover of any given impulse.

But to try to disentangle the motives of each impulse would cause more trouble than advantage, and the attempted dissociation would give us nothing but an intellectual analysis, which is the opposite of what we want.

Increase of awareness must be attained by watchfulness, but without tension. And watchfulness does not mean introspection.

Watchfulness means not to be asleep. Yet the preoccupations of the daily round are apt to keep us so absorbed, to the detriment of our inner life, that often the awakening of our conscousness is the last thing we think about. And thus for lack of watchfulness we are really in a state of sleep, however intense our intellectual or professional activity may be; for without paying attention we cannot have any contact with the two witnesses, which give us the evidence of our real being.

If we want our Permanent Witness to make us truly aware of our physical, emotional, and mental states, we must pay it constant attention, and carefully observe the behavior of our Automaton.

This watchfulness would soon become tedious if there were no enlivening interest to justify it. For this reason it is frequently necessary to give a little time to "mediation," by which is meant a state of meditation designed to arouse us from our sleepy unawareness. The term "mediation" is used rather than "meditation" to avoid the error of interpreting the latter in the sense of mental reflection, or equally of spiritual meditation.

The state to be aimed at is a state of mediation between the Automaton and Permanent Witness, and appeals to the latter to observe and regulate prudently the harmony of the organic functions of the former. It is a mediation because it is a state which mediates between thought and intuition, the attention being concentrated on that part of one's being of which one wishes to become aware.

This "mediation" requires physical and mental calm and relaxation. It begins with thought, which must call to mind the organs in the area under consideration; but if the "mediation" is well managed, thought will gradually give way and allow the intuition to reveal the vital knowledge that it discovers. This knowledge is simply the awakening of an innate consciousness, brought about by concentration of attention on a given region.

The subjects on which it will be useful to practice mediation are those outlined in Chapter 3. In brief, they are these:

First, the four physical bodies (the bones, the flesh, the vessels, the nerves); it is a good practice to visualize these frequently in order to understand the part that each plays in the harmony of the whole.

Second, the organic groups, which establish an interaction of influence between their constituent members.* These are:

• The Tree of Exchange, which, by inhalation and exhalation of what Hippocrates calls "the airs and waters," establishes a relation between the organic and animal life of the human egg and that of the Cosmic Egg

• The seven essential functions, each ruling a group of four organs that have a relative of sympathy on account of their functional identity

• The four regions, whose orientation affects the character of the organs they include.

Finally, there are the four functional principles of these regions:

• In the upper region, the lungs, which revitalize the blood and are the

_____
*See Appendix I.

seat of the vital spirits and of the unconscious vital urge of the cells and the Automaton

• In the lower region, the small intestine, which is the body's principal feeder, since it selects the nourishing ingredients from the food and renders them assimilable

• In the left region, the stomach, which "opens the way" to the functions of digestion (whose final product will enrich the blood) and which for this reason is called in ancient Egypt "the mouth of the heart"

• In the right region, the liver, in which personal characteristics are recorded, the seat of the Personal vital urge, the organ which responds to the Permanent Witness.

Daily mediation can be performed on any of these subjects, and the result will be a gradually increased mastery of the conscious "I" over the Automaton.

Success will depend upon assiduity.

Although this mediation has a physical object, it influences the subtler states nonetheless, for there are no watertight doors between matter and energy. The analytical picture only exists in our brains; life works as a synthesis, and becomes clear to the seeker who does not dissect its workings and dissociate them.

There are three advantages, then, to this kind of mediation: first, it is a gradual training in the awakening of the subtler states, using a physical reference point and thus avoiding the risk of psychic illusions; second, the gleams of higher consciousness which it arouses will make it easier to distinguish true intuitions from fantasies; and third, the seeker who applies this mediation to his organic functions will rise above his animal self and become a conscious being.

The principal obstacle to acquiring this degree of control is that the Personality resists it with intellectual criticism and all the aggressiveness of the bile, and for this reason one must learn to break the circuit between the brain and the gallbladder.

Most organic troubles are caused by emotion, apprehension, humiliation, and in general by thoughts and acts which offend the personal will and the impulses of passion. The reaction is aggravated by tightening of the nervous plexuses, but the organic starting point of these troubles is almost always in the functioning of the bile or of the brain. The bile may be disturbed by a vexatious thought or by an impulse of irritation arising in the liver (which is the seat of the personality), but the result either way is the same; the bile-brain circuit goes into action instantaneously, the bile irritating the brain and the brain exciting the bile, and the resulting two-way current sets off a chain reaction through the system: bile—brain —bile—stomach—spleen—bile, and so on. A few drops of bile in the stomach can be the beginning of pain and trouble, which could have been avoided by prompt intervention.

The first thing to do is to break the circuit between bile and brain by resolutely turning one's thoughts away from the vexatious subject. This does not mean finding convincing arguments, but simply breaking off the contact by, for example, forcing oneself to careful observation of some object or other. When the train of thought has thus been redirected, a few moments of mediation will prevent the reaction of the bile from continuing.

This small act of control has the highest importance, for it ensures that when the anarchistic Automaton attacks the conscious self, victory shall go to the latter.

16

Conduct

It is important to discern which of the various elements in one's life and makeup are relative and which are real. This is the knowledge needed in order not to die altogether.

The important thing is to rouse oneself from sleep and no longer be the victim of the habitual impulses and actions of the Automaton, but to let the conscious Self control them constantly.

In other words, nothing can save us from the loss of free will unless the Permanent Witness is awakened and kept continually watchful. This, however, will set us free to control our thoughts and actions in accordance with the aim suggested by the Spiritual Witness. Such control is evidence of the presence of the Spirit, and without it our experience on earth will miss its aim.

The first stage in taking control of the Automaton is to stop the tyranny of habit and the waste of vital force. Vital force is precious and should not be expended thoughtlessly. One can economize it by avoiding futile talk and argument, useless preoccupations, and unnecessary violent movements. Actions should be carefully watched to prevent their becoming automatic, and one should have the courage to alter one's way of doing them temporarily and from time to time. The limbs should be trained to independent movement, so that they can perform different actions simultaneously.

Equally, the many and various aspects of the ego should not be allowed to impose their incoherent wills and prejudices. Watch yourself acting, and dare to decide in your conscious ''I'' what type of thought and behavior is most in accordance with your real aim at the moment.

If your ultimate aim is the result of a decision in principle, your immediate aim will gradually change as the enlargement of your awareness sheds more light upon it. In this does experience consist, and for this reason is constant watchfulness indispensable, for you must be continuously aware of how the Duel is going and the condition of the combatants.

Watch the phases of your liberation, and refuse to be the slave of your likes and dislikes, or of what you think impossible, for to break a habit is to release oneself from a bond. But equally one must not become a slave to watchfulness! Self-analysis is not the answer, nor is a paroxysm of will power made musclebound by fear of failure.

Watchfulness means truthful observance of the motives of our actions. It means remaining in constant contact with the Spiritual Heart, which is the seat of the Spiritual Witness and the source of discernment.

There are three realms on which we must keep watch: the physical, the emotional, and the mental. The methods already described will work together to control thought and emotion. The organic functions must be regarded as animal forces and treated as a skilful trainer treats wild animals, without violence, but without carelessness, and without allowing them to have whims.

To train them without risk of revolt, the trainer must be quite certain of the superiority of human over animal force; for the slightest doubt of this will put him in danger. He must know, however, that he communicates with his animals not by willpower under the direction of intellect, but by his innate instinctive consciousness of the own lower natures. This is the only way to control them wisely and not by violence.

And this is exactly the method that man must use to control his own animal organism. The Personal Consciousness must rule the organic functions and actually control them, not be their slave; for wretched slavery is all the ego gets in return for its anxiety and preoccupation with "my bad digestion," "my weak heart," "my poor stomach," and so forth.

Our physical organs (and this cannot be too often repeated) are animal forces, which will quite naturally obey a man who is prepared to command them. They are there to serve him, not to enslave him. But the ego is so lazy that it makes him quite glad to abdicate this power in return for the secret satisfaction of pitying his own sufferings, or of attracting attention to his pathetic case. Most of our pathological conditions are aggravated by this unconfessed indulgence. The same applies to our personal dramas and daily worries; we should have the courage to admit that they feed largely on the pity of others, and on our own. In most cases, what would be left of them if we passed them over in total silence?

But the two Egos, the Personal and the Automatic, when they want to attract attention and excuse their egoism, have the cunning of the serpent.

The centripetal force of the Ego is immeasurable. It simply is centripetal force, and every human Self will remain its slave until its own sun shall draw it into the light.

For this reason the Way of the Heart is the only way to final liberation.

The second stage is to awaken the intuitive consciousness which makes it possible for a man to unite himself with the cosmic soul. One who wishes to attain this will not spend time on the details of color, scent and form, which so agreeably satisfy the desires of the senses, but will listen within himself to the reverberation of the vital forces of Nature.

The autumn's wine develops a kind of fever in the spring, when the sap is rising in its original stock, and it is said to "weep the tears of the vine," and also to "be aware of its mother." Man too, without knowing it, is aware of his mother, instinctive Nature, being subject to her seasons and urges, her cycles and accidents.

One can be subject to these either instinctively or consciously. In this connection "instinctively" means obeying the innate instinctive consciousness without allowing brain-consciousness to stifle it with conventional notions and traditional prudery. To follow this line is to follow the natural course of life-experience, by which a man evolves toward his goal, slowly, perhaps, but without going astray. Mental prudery prevents this experience and delays his evolution considerably.

One submits consciously, however, if one develops concurrently the double consciousness both of the Personal and the Spiritual Self.

To achieve this, one must take care every day, as the Egyptian ritual so beautifully expressed it, to "give the house to its master." This means that after awakening functional awareness of the organs by concentration without tension,* one must practice an intense "mediation of the heart"** in order to give the Spiritual Consciousness full control over the Automaton and the Conscious "I."

This is a rapid path of development by which instinct leads on to intuitive knowledge, automatic behavior is replaced by watchfulness, and so man discovers the possibility of a higher state.

This higher state is one of serenity in which the personal will no longer resists the impulses of the heart, and where that "free will," of which the self-conscious ego is so proud, will be replaced by discrimination between the relative and the real, with the freedom of choice which this confers. So ends the conflict between intellect and intuitive perception. There follows an attentive silence, in which man asks himself: "What do I really know?" Thus he becomes able to recognize his Master.

*See Chapter 15.
**See Chapters 7 and 15.

Who is your Master?

He can only be the one who knows the plan of your destiny and can unerringly lead you to its fulfillment. He cannot in fact be other than the Permanent Witness of your destiny, your own imperishable consciousness, that is, your Spiritual Witness enriched by the experience of the Permanent Witness. It is the element of Christ in you, which alone can be the mediator between you as a human being and the divine motive-power which your intellect cannot grasp.

This witness is your Master because it is your Truth, what you truly are, your own true Way and indestructible Life. What else can be the meaning of St. Paul's words: "Until Christ be formed in you" (Galatians 4:19)?

If you have heard the Master's call, do not make the mistake of seeking the light up in the clouds and refusing to look at the darkness out of which it is born. It is born in darkness through the development of consciousness, which makes the darkness able to recognize it. There is, however, a danger that one may stifle it under false illuminations and illusions about oneself.

One must explore one's darkness in order to find what shocks will make the light shine out of it. But if you are afraid to stir up the mud that you really are, you will stay stuck in it. And if you are afraid to face your ingrained habits and illusions, you will lose the path to the Master and have to endure the bumps of the path that you have chosen.

If you fear to break down your obstacles, you will never attain the suprahuman state. But this breakage does not mean renunciation and resignation; that would produce not life but inertia and death.

The force of a repressed desire may return to haunt you in dreams, for it is only restrained, not redirected; but if the quest for the higher joy becomes intense enough, you will forget the lower.

Never be resigned! That is only a sign of impotence. Have the courage rather to increase your suffering until it sublimates itself into an ardor of attainment.

Always avoid mediocrity, with its petty anemic virtues, its barren regrets, and its efforts so soon exhausted. Good intentions are unavailing in hours of crisis; to advance one must leap directly!

Our different states of consciousness are evoked haphazardly by the movement of life, but, not wishing to separate them too rigidly, we shall try to arouse awareness of them by methods appropriate to each. The subjects will be the same, but looked at from a different point of view, as if they were observed in a different atmosphere and—be it remembered—not so much understood as experienced.

So we shall now begin to speak a different language. We have done our best for comprehension on the rational level, but now the time has come for direct communication between two living beings, without concern for "I," "you," or "the other." All communication, after all, is Consciousness awakening another consciousness. So as we watch together let "you" listen to yourself.

The great magician on this path is our own inner attitude, but it can only accomplish miracles if it is put into practice instead of remaining a dream and an ideal.

There is not much to do, but a good deal to prevent.

There are no beliefs to adopt, but many to abandon.

The aim is to see Reality, to hear with the inward ear, and to act with awareness.

There are seven obstacles to be eliminated, and seven accomplishments to attain.

PART THREE

17

The Seven Accomplishments

THE SENSE OF PRESENCE

The first of the essential accomplishments is the "sense of Presence."

Most men today know nothing of their body except its needs and illnesses, and restrict their consciousness to the brain. The intellect, busy with daily cares, demands the right to decide all actions, even in physical, emotional, and spiritual matters, and never thinks of asking whether this demand is fair or merely arbitrary. The head is in such a whirl of thoughts that it can attend to nothing else, and if it takes any notice of the rest of the body, that is only for reasons of health, vanity, or sensuality. Man's higher being is regarded as an intruder, excluded from any vital contact, and requested to restrict its Presence to the rare occasions set aside for it—if there are any!

What are the consequences of this misdirection?

When attention is fixed on any part of the body, that part becomes a magnet for energy. But intellectual attention carries back all sensation to the terminus in the brain, leaving the rest of the body emptied of awareness; for mental energy cannot enliven the other vital centers, so they remain flaccid and unable to attract their proper share of the subtle energy, or vital fire.

It is this energy, however, which revitalizes. It alone can give the vitality to overcome illness and even to arouse our higher perceptions. The greatest obstacle to its penetration throughout the body is the "thought factory," whose infernal machinery drowns our sense of Presence.

This Presence is the immanence of our true being; so in this sense one cannot speak of a Presence except in a creature having in it something immortal, which is, in man, the higher consciousness.

Since the Consciousness has two aspects—the ''I'' Consciousness or Permanent Witness, and the Spiritual Consciousness, or Spiritual Witness—we can also speak of two aspects of the Presence. And so to have the sense of Presence means to be aware of either one of the two, the Personal Presence or the Spiritual Presence. If both are united under control of the Spiritual Witness, then we have a real presence of the divine, a realization of our indestructible being (the Christ or Horus in us).

The whole of this study has been a preparation for the achievement of this union, and all the effort given to it can now find a direct response in the comfort of this Presence, which, as soon as it even begins to manifest, is the best answer to the great question: ''What's the use?''

Learn to listen to its voice and it will solve the problems of your life. It is your only Reality, yet you stifle it by rationalizations and petty worries.

This is the Presence to which the sages and the evangelists refer when they speak of the need to be watchful, that the Master when he comes may not find the lamp unlit.

Learn to watch, instead of accepting the illusions created by the agitation of daily life and the activity of the brain, for despite appearances they will leave you in a state of slumber unless your higher consciousness is awakened. But this watchfulness does not depend on will or reason.

The aim is to experience life like a warm energy filling the whole body as water fills a sponge.

The aim is to be aware of the whole organism and know it to be obedient to the discipline imposed by the Conscious Self.

The aim is to accept the heart's arbitrament on all troubles caused by impulses of the personality.

The aim is to keep your eye on the compass and hold the tiller steady, whatever the violence of the elements.

Learn first to be the consciousness of your own machinery. Then feel in yourself the confidence of the crew in the captain's watchfulness. Finally become the captain's consciousness, silently detecting the least reactions of ship and crew.

Then at last you will know the joy of escape. Certain henceforward of your direction, you can see your route disappear on the horizon, and the horizon lose itself in the sky, and you will become the consciousness of the infinite.

CONCENTRATION

However great a person's intelligence, his effectiveness will always be in proportion to his power of concentration. If his energy be dispersed over various objectives, he will never produce a great achievement.

But the attainment of the suprahuman state is the greatest of all achievements; so if it is not the greatest of all preoccupations, one might as well not attempt it.

In the present teaching the principle has been to group tendencies together and direct them with a view to concentrating on this point. Such a constant return to essentials should be helpful, and one should resist the inertia which tries to excuse itself with a variety of distractions. The principal ally of inertia is that debauchment of thought which incessantly seizes on every impulse as an opportunity of distraction, to satisfy its "love of variety," and thus weakens your inner force. Until this joyride can be brought under control there is no hope of any far-reaching results.

One must be able to outface the wandering tendency of thought, holding to one's direction in spite of it, and if it appears incorrigible one can usefully follow the course of the thought backward and discover its origin. This effort of attention increases one's power of concentration, and shows the mind who is its master.

This, however, is only a mechanical procedure which uses thought for the control of thought. Nevertheless it is better than a tense effort of will, or a more or less hypnotic concentration on some picture or object.

One should avoid techniques for concentrating the willpower. Willpower is a natural force, and its faculty is to impose its own authority, by compulsion if need be. With a strong effort of concentration a man can even exteriorize his willpower and cause it to act on others. But such action by force is in opposition to the Way of the Heart.

For the will is an agent of the Personality only.

The Heart's agent is the magnetic power which attracts and holds a man's vital forces within the sphere and rhythm of his own inner sun. It is in fact his affinity with his Spiritual Self, which can give him courage to overcome the resistances of the Personality.

When his impulses are at one with the physical and spiritual harmony of his being, that is the Wisdom of the Heart. And if its suggestions are accepted, the result is a desire to transcend oneself, to yield to this attraction so dreaded by the Ego, to be carried away toward a higher destiny and convert one's as-yet-unformulated yearning into an effective force.

If this force is to be made real, it must be the object on which concentration is focused. All other attractions and personal wills are distractions and diminish its potency.

Concentration is quite a different thing from willpower; the two must not be confused.

The concentration to be aimed at is a convergence of all the vital energies on the ideal goal, transforming it into a powerful magnet, just as rays of light focused by a lens transform their focal point into a source of fire.

When this general concentration of life has been achieved, one will be able to concentrate attention in a similar manner on every act and gesture, without needing to employ the will.

Concentration is a double-edged weapon. Used with a taut effort of will, it distracts one from the Way of the Heart; but used with a desire to pursue that way, it leads to simplicity of heart and thought and viewpoint.

Try, therefore, to simplify the path.

The goal is before you; approach it without looking back. To wallow in the past is to turn oneself into a pillar of salt.

So prune away superfluous details, and do not dwell on unhelpful memories. Refuse to respond to worry and vain regrets, and avoid useless words, thinking rather of the true meaning of the word.

Concentration requires simplification; so concentration will help to attain simplicity of heart.

SERENITY

The weather is called serene when no clouds darken the sky and neither wind nor fog disturbs the transparency of the air.

The sky in man is the subtle sphere or aura which surrounds and penetrates him, and in which his own luminaries perform their revolutions. It is the atmosphere created by the emanations of his organs and other constituent elements, which radiate and receive their subtle fluidic influences.

The Heart is the sun which illumines the sphere of man.

The serenity of his sky comes from the harmony of his inner forces, and the transparency of his Light is the result of nonresistance.

To acquire serenity one must first eliminate certain weaknesses of the human animal, namely nervous impatience, instinctive haste, and instability. These three defects are the result of an erroneous notion of values, which in turn is derived from a hybrid and ill-directed consciousness, half animal and half human.

A man not yet enlightened by his Spiritual Witness regarding real and relative values will let his intellect defend the instinctive desires of his lower self, and their disorderly demands will create crosscurrents of impatience, haste, and incoherent caprice.

In giving in to these impulses the human Automaton resembles certain types of animal. The dog, for example, quivers with impatience at the sight of a juicy bone. The monkey, with its perpetual distractions, typifies instability and dispersion of thought. The fly by its agitation throws itself into the spider's web. Haste is exemplified in the bee's care for its social duty, and the anxiety of the ant, which always has something to do, but in doing it hurries into unnecessary detours, knowing the right direction but not knowing how to surmount the obstacles.

Other animals give us a lesson in self-control: the cat, for instance, whose wisdom is a model because it combines the most intent passion with the calmest indifference. Motionless it plans its leap, and performs it exactly; the strength of its muscles is matched by its relaxation in repose; in sleep it has the abandon of an infant, yet its instinct is ever alert; it can fall without danger because it does not resist; hunting and fighting are games of pure pleasure for it, it hunts with rancor and plays without an object; it is ever ready to attack without animosity, and to defend itself without apprehension; being indifferent to victory, it cannot feel defeat.

Serenity comes from independence.

This independence, to be created in oneself, is not indifference, but neutrality with regard to the impressions received from without—whether pretty or ugly, good or bad, happy or sad, pleasant or unpleasant. It is one thing to observe these qualities and quite another to let them affect our moods.

If our evaluation of them is based on personal preference, then we cannot discern the real. We must practice the discrimination of real and relative values by means of neutrality, which is the first step toward "transparency."

Concentrating upon essential values will open the door to this discrimination. And the attainment of the sense of Presence will close the door to illusory values. This gradual purification is the key to transparency.

Transparency is the quality of letting the light pass through one, the limpid neutrality which lets objects be seen through it undeformed.

The same definition describes the state of man who is transparent to the Light and open to the Presence.

This transparency becomes illumination within and radiance without. It does not prevent the selfish assaults of the Ego, but it weakens them.

Peace on earth cannot mean the suppression of the opposing forces, but their reconciliation in working for a common aim, which is indestructible life.

As you struggle with yourself for your independence, you cannot eradicate your own resistances, but you can avoid the conditions which favor them. Avoid therefore all conditions which disturb the serenity of your sky. Do not let it ever be disturbed: either by the turbulence of the brain, which opens the door to your bad angel; or by pessimism and doubt, which quench the kindling fire; or by fear under whatever name—anxiety, scruples, caution—for that dries up the heart and extinguishes the flame of Love.

THE APPROPRIATE GESTURE

The fourth accomplishment is knowledge of the appropriate gesture. Once again the sense of Presence will teach us how to attain it; and it should be our care in every action.

The absence of it corresponds to the state described commonly as ''lack of presence of mind.'' Really, one should think more often of the meaning of that expression; for what will be the use of an act performed without the mind being present?

Distraction has become too facile an excuse for unthinking behavior; it ought rather to be regarded as the loss of a moment out of one's life. Our conscious ''I'' should be an ever-alert witness of all our acts and gestures, for it has the immortal memory of the awareness that we acquire in performing them, whereas our intellectual memory is unreliable and cannot outlast the brain.

Thus any act of ours that goes unnoticed by this witness is lost to our vital experience; but if we perform it with awareness, it enriches our true Knowledge.

One cannot hope to find Knowledge and at the same time ignore matter; and the basis of the knowledge of matter is the appropriate gesture.

To know the appropriate gesture in any handicraft is to know how a given material can be worked. To know the appropriate gesture of an animal or plant is to know its appetites, its astral signature, and its particular qualities. To know the appropriate gesture of any genesis is to know the laws of Becoming of the world.

The first degree of skill is to practice the most direct and exact gesture for producing the required effect. Whether one is opening a lock or cultivating a plant, casting iron or baking a cake, the appropriate gesture is always equally important because it obliges one to understand the nature of the material on which one works.

Nature is not to be understood by a theoretical knowledge of chemistry, geology or mechanics; it must be studied in the actual materials, for by their affinities, by their formal analogies and conditions of transformation, they will reveal their place in the terrestrial system and the secrets of their becoming.

No amount of intellectual learning will produce this result; one must make contact oneself with each single substance, and experience in oneself its transformations, resistances, and weaknesses.

An experienced blacksmith can tell without any exterior sign the point at which the metal will break; and an enameler must be able to tell the state of fusion of his enamel without taking it out of the oven to look, or his labor will be wasted.

The slightest direct experience, thus acquired, is more than all theoretical learning of the subject.

Thus, whatever your profession may be, watch and try out the "appropriate gestures" of several practitioners, in order to see how different materials react. Sharpen your sensibility by trying to find the most perfect way of working the material as you wish. And do not regret the time given to this ancillary work, for this "wasted" time will be of inestimable value. Do not try to give it a utilitarian interest; forget the bourgeois sense of earthly values. Take pleasure in refining your sensibility and opening your inner senses to that which your thinking faculty cannot penetrate. You will soon notice that this switchover is already opening to you the first door of Knowledge.

Assiduous practice in searching for the appropriate gesture teaches one the rhythm and character of things, and the supreme degree of it is identification, or perfect communion with the thing in question.

This, according to Lao-tse, is the Knowledge of Tao, the union of the knower with the known.

There is a fine Taoist image which gives one a notion of one's progress. The swimmer who can swim calmly across the river is a good swimmer: the swimmer who can swim through the rapids is a very good swimmer: but the perfect swimmer, the practitioner of Tao, is he who can jump in the river and let the whirlpools seize him and cast him up without losing his serenity.

SILENCE

Silence is the earliest fruit to ripen when you have learned control of the senses and of the three lower states, the physical, emotional, and mental. It is the well of wisdom containing all treasures, the locus of all knowledge.

Nature abhors a vacuum; hence when illusion disappears, reality takes its place.

Our five senses explore the realm of appearances; they are windows open on the destructible world, and to be able to enter the interior palace we must be capable of closing them at will.

This palace of silence, or temple of contemplation, has been enthusiastically described in all initiatory literature, for it allows us, once the lower worlds have been controlled, to penetrate one after another the higher states or worlds.

All mystical teachings agree that "The empty shall be filled," as

Lao-tse says; that "He who has little shall receive much." "Vomit your thinking," Lao-tse says again; and "Blessed are the poor in spirit, for theirs is the kingdom of heaven"; and the Kingdom of Heaven, says the Nazarene Master, is for little children and those who resemble them.

It is in Silence, devoid of appearances, that Reality is manifested. That is the one Temple of which all others are only likenesses; and in it the essence of all religions is identical in this proposition:

"The causal Spirit, becoming conscious of itself, creates the forms or appearances through which it returns to its origin as the Universal Consciousness."

The first form of Silence is immobility: immobility of thought and no will to action; immobility of body and no will to emotion. (This second prevents the danger of psychic illusions during meditation.) Psychic images, or visions, are a danger, the more so since the beginner takes them for a privilege and a sign of progress. They are, on the contrary, the mirages of an unhealthy country that one should hastily avoid. All hallucinations and ecstatic dreaming should be put aside, and one should be continuously conscious of the desire not to be deceived by cerebral or psychic tricks of imagination.

Perfect Silence should be the aim.

Entering into the Silence should be like entering a deep cave; the sounds and voices from outside become more distant, so too should all memories and intellectual notions; the ear should become closed to well-known voices and forget even the forms of language which have been the mold of thought.

By caring for an ill-founded aestheticism the decadent languages of modern times have lost the sense of initiation and the magic of the Word, and one must become detached from their present factitious forms before one can rediscover the true feeling for the Word. Conventional thoughts only prevent one from understanding the Word that has no form and the Voice which has no sound, which speaks only in Silence.

Understanding is the perception of the consciousness of the soul, the exercise of the intuition, the opening of the inward ear, and it alone can reveal the vital meaning of anything. It requires Silence as the embryo requires the womb.

Its seat is the central region near the heart. This is the true solar heart of our body. There we listen and feel the growth of that which is learnt in Silence.

One must listen to the Silence, even if nothing speaks and nothing answers, even if everything in one seems stupid and inert.

Silence is always fruitful, but its fruit often appears outside one's periods of silence, at the most unexpected moments.

Silence is the well into which falls the universe, the void into which the Spirit is drawn. But the Consciousness which is aroused at such moments may remain obscure for a while longer, and the Wisdom which they bring forth in the depths of the heart may take time to rise to the surface. And, while we wait, futile preoccupations may stifle it.

One must learn therefore to incubate this treasure. It would be extravagant to expect that one should immediately comprehend to the full a thought conceived in the short time set aside from daily cares.

The first result will be a vague awareness that some new understanding or other is not far off. Be grateful for it, for ingratitude and skepticism are a bar to progress. Wait patiently while the confused lights settle into plain evidence. And do not try to hasten the process or make it more exact by intellectual deduction, for that only prevents the development of intuition.

Any Knowledge which the Heart obtains will rise to the surface like the cream on milk, without the least effort of thought; and that is true intuitive knowledge.

Only after that can the intellect of the brain take it over and tie it up with what it already knows. This is a translation of the originally intuitive conception, and it requires one to practice listening with the inward ear, in an impersonal, neutral, docile state of mind, for the corrections suggested by the Wisdom of the Heart.

The obstacles to the growth of intuitive knowledge are:
• Eagerness for results
• Use of the imagination, whether intellectually or emotionally
• Intrusion of irrelevant thoughts during meditation
• Ingratitude and skepticism when intuitive perceptions cannot yet be understood intellectually
• Self-complacency and unwillingness to confess mistakes.

It is important to realize the principle that "Everything is in man" and there is nothing in Nature which is not represented in man; but over and above Nature a seed of Divine Light has been given to him, as man, to bring to fruition.

Genius is only a momentary rending of the veil that hides this Light. The veil is woven of our habits and prejudices, our personal likes and dislikes, our ambition and personal will, and our vain pride in rational knowledge.

The voice of the Light is the consciousness of the universe. When a man has broken the shell of his ego, there is no problem that it will not solve for him.

The ability to hear this voice is in proportion to the simplicity and "transparency" of the listener.

THANKFULNESS

To clarify what is meant here by thankfulness we must consider the subjects to which it should apply; we must decide what impressions and perceptions are to be noted and intensified because they have a vital and real value, and distinguish them from those whose value is uncertain or only relative.

Our senses are receiving stations which transmit to the brain information regarding the appearances of things in terms of sight, touch, hearing, taste, and smell. The brain translates and records these with such faculties as it has; that is, it defines, classifies, and values the impressions received according to two principles: association of ideas and comparison with previous notions.

Beyond this its experience cannot go, for its power of judgment is restricted by the quantity and exactness of the notions it already possesses; and these in turn depend on the acuteness of its sense-perceptions and the faithfulness of its records. In other words, they are always relative, since they are always affected by the personality of the percipient.

With the inner sense this is not so. They can enter into direct contact with the essence and rhythm of things, by tuning, or synchronizing, that faculty in the observer which is identical in the thing observed.

Thus there are two opposite patterns of life, which evoke opposite reflexes:

Sense-perception is brought from outside by the five senses, and the tendency of the "sensory" man will always be to expand his life and joy outside himself.

But all true Knowledge comes from within, and the "meditative" man will find his strength by concentrating his vital force and joy within himself.

A feeling violently expressed is soon exhausted; but a sorrow brooded over in secret may take root and become the cause of an incurable disease.

Joy brooded over in silence becomes a source of intense heat, like a fire covered with ashes. Joy is an emotional expansion of the sensitive fibers of one's being, which open themselves in order to better experience the object or cause of their exaltation.

But the springs of human joy are almost always poisoned by possessiveness; and the joy of possession is restricted by the object possessed and by the fear of losing it.

Possession is a form of satisfaction, and satisfaction is akin to satiety and saturation, which do not imply joy; for in joy there is an element of power. So if desire is an exaltation of power, then its satisfacton is a lowering of tension, a weakening.

Joy is an exalting sensation of expansion, the enlargement of the heart; its absence is an inert condition in which fear can easily be born; and fear is a contraction, the opposite of expansion.

Expansion is a state of serene confidence, it gives the impression of ease and liberty, and one breathes freely. Conversely, to breathe freely and deeply increases the vital force, and in turn this increase gives an exaltation which leads to joy.

So joy is an essential element in the mastery of human life, and one should learn to cultivate it as a real fountain of vitality.

The richness of any joy is always multiplied by being grateful for it, and that is why one should develop the sense of thankfulness.

For to acknowledge a thing with thankfulness is to let it reverberate through one's being and arouse there its own vibrations. To acknowledge a thing learned or received is to reflect it within oneself, and the reflection multiplies its value.

But there are two ways of reflecting the Light: One is the way of inanimate things, which, like a mirror reflect outward a light fainter than they receive; the other is the way of living seed and organic matter, which concentrate the light within themselves and bring it to fruition.

The thinking brain is a mirror of the world; it reflects energy outward in the form of mental projections and fugitive thoughts, but these reflected waves contain no spiritual seed or vitalizing power.

And emotion, if brought into contact with the intellect for purposes of verification, at once loses its character, and the vitalizing quality of its original impulse is destroyed.

Just as energy is perceptible to us either as movement or as condensed into phenomenal objects, so too can emotion be canalized in different directions. It may be no more than an intellectual and therefore artificial reaction if confined to the mode of expression of the memory and the brain; but it can also become a vitalizing power if attended to with the inward ear and if its repercussions are allowed to spread freely through the centers of vital energy.

Joy, therefore, to enhance its power, should be met with thankfulness for its vitalizing quality.

There are thousands of opportunities for real joy which can spread vitalizing vibrations through anyone who pays attention to them: the perception, for instance, of a pure work of art, the beauty of an appropriate gesture, a sudden moment of awareness, a sorrow overcome, the sudden shock that shows us the reality of a value.

And yet man feels that he owes it to his self-respect to stifle his emotions and deny his sensibilities, or even, out of avarice, to see how much they are worth and try to make some utilitarian profit out of them.

He who, like a child or a primitive, can let the vivifying flood flow into him, and concentrate it like a wise man in his heart, has found a secret fountain of life.

For joy is a great treasure, and of incalculable power.

Joy multiplied by thankfulness becomes a center of attraction for benefic vital forces, for its waves, being warm and altruistic, attract others of a like nature, just as gloom attracts harmful vibrations and unhealthy forces.

Deliberately nothing is said here of gratitude in the moral sense of thankfulness to a benefactor, for the fully conscious man has a different point of view from that of the "herd-soul." When a benefit received is of a material order, it amounts to a material debt, which the wise man will settle on that plane, in a spirit of justice and on account of karma. But if it is of a spiritual order it will count as a joy to be welcomed and reflected on with love; for this inward reflection is the best form of gratitude to the benefactor, since in the spiritual realm a treasure is always shared between giver and receiver, simply because of the offered Light being accepted and cultivated.

Ingratitude, in such a case, would consist in refusing to accept the Light, or in claiming all merit for it oneself. This cannot harm the giver, but is its own punishment, since such egoism obscures the Light and cuts off contact with its source.

GENEROSITY

Generosity, in the highest human sense of the word, means forgetting oneself for the sake of another. In the suprahuman sense, it is the union of the Personal Self with the impersonal Universal Self.

The distinction between the animal man and the fully conscious man is that between egoism and altruism.

The earthly meaning of generosity is egoistic, for a person can only give that which belongs to him as his own (that is, his goods or his person), but in giving these there is always a reflex of self-interest; in fact ultimately one gives for one's own sake. In giving alms to a beggar we satisfy our feeling of pity, or else we acquire merit, or, to take it on the highest level, we offer help to a portion of our own common humanity; a gift made to one's "own" son is made to one's own flesh; a gift to a friend expects friendship in return; a gift to the mighty or to the gods invokes a favor in return; and our chances of receiving the favor are always greater, the more nearly the value of our gift corresponds to the wishes of our patron.

This is pure calculating egotism!

In our egotism we lose the idea of indestructible values and judge all the worlds by our own measure, observing them through the prism of our feelings.

We credit the heavenly powers with human appetites, and so lose our sense of the "divine appetite," the appetite for heavenly things.

The first form of this "divine appetite" is altruism, the sense of true generosity.

A gift given in the hope of receiving something, even if only gratitude or "merit," is not a gift but an exchange or loan, a commercial transaction. All human gifts presuppose such an exchange, for earthly values imply the idea of comparison, balance, and compensation.

This law of compensation is one of the most tyrannical conditions of the lower states of being; with the regularity of a pendulum it equalizes the level between the two intercommunicating vessels. It is the basis of the ideas of offering and libation to the gods—tithes, first fruits of flocks, herds, and harvest, the first drops of wine, and so forth. One shares with Nature or the gods, by way of compensation, the fruits they have given.

Thus human generosity always creates a debt; or if it is the discharge of a debt it becomes a burden on the receiver.

The Gospel advises us not to let the left hand know what the right hand hath given; but even this is only an effort in the right direction, for the duality remains; and if duality remains, the need for compensation remains.

True generosity is that which gives itself without compensation.

Only the Spirit can give and receive in this absolute sense; for its generosity is total, that is to say it amounts to a fusion of giver and receiver, without any diminution of the self.

For this reason the sense of true generosity is a divine sense; for only the divine element in man can conceive it and bring it to fruition.

For it alone can awaken the Cosmic Consciousness in a man, can exalt him beyond his own limits until he transcends the bounds of possibility, until his thirst for the Infinite becomes so great that he becomes like it and can give himself as it does in an irreversible act of radiance.

This is the royal generosity of the Sun.

Once you have felt the call of Immensity, the thrill of the Unknown which is felt as knowable, you know quite well that you will never be able to quench your longing for it, however much common life may drown it under a flood of banalities. And once you have known the fire of love for it, even if only for a moment, you have within you a spark capable of burning up every obstacle to the realization of your true Power. For the Power of the Self is unlimited, and only the Ego resists this power of the impersonal Self.

The union of the two is an irresistible Love in which Height and Depth are united, in which they know not that they "give" themselves to each other, since their giving is a fusion, a rejoicing in Love, an ardent vibration; there is no longer any comparison, no longer any compensation; no longer "I" or "Thou," but only an intensity of Life in which all is mutual penetration and mutual knowledge.

18

The Seven Obstacles

The obstacles which delay our realization of the suprahuman state are of two types.

In mankind as a whole there are the dispositions which impede the honest prosecution of a quest, and these are the seven obstacles to be considered in this chapter. But there are also the resistances inherent in the character of the individual, which we commonly call his faults.

Among faults some can be eliminated by care and perseverance; those, that is, which are due to bad education or immediate heredity—we say "immediate" because the effects of remote heredity are different; it may happen that a person is a reincarnation of his distant ancestor. Other faults are the bad effects of the astrological influences which each receives at birth. These astrological signatures, together with man's innate tendencies, constitute the profound nature or rhythms of the individual; they cannot be eliminated, but it is possible to reorient them toward the better aspect of the quality or tendency from which they originate.

This will mean that their object and mode of action must be altered. For example, the anger and aggressiveness of Mars can be transformed into courage and joy in "sacrifice." The sensuality of Venus can be used to direct sense-impressions toward the cultivation of an impersonal artistic sense; the love of sensual pleasure will then gradually diminish as the wisdom of the vivifying fire burns brighter.

The Mercurian's instability and restless activity, and his delight in cunning for its own sake, can be transformed into understanding of motives, or dexterity in learning the appropriate gestures of a craft.

When his sense of responsibility is aroused, the pride and vanity of the Jupiter type will be changed into generosity.

The selfish pessimism of the Saturnian can lead to silent meditation and the study of profounder causes, and so become a source of wisdom.

Instead of apathy and nonchalance, the cold Lunar person can learn that deliberate passivity which, when combined with emotional neutrality, opens the door to intuition.

The ambitious and dominating nature of the Solar man can be transformed into the expansiveness of impersonal Love, which only develops its power of attraction in order to better radiate selflessly to others.

Excuses are the first obstacle to getting rid of all these obstacles—the perpetual excuses invented by the Personality to justify its weaknesses.

So long as we excuse ourselves, no transformation is possible. No light will shine through the veil of illusions which these predudices are always weaving for us.

There can be no possibility of discernment if we blind ourselves with continual excuses. The prerequisite to the awakening of our higher consciousness is a true knowledge of our own tendencies, and how can we attain that if we misrepresent our motives by putting forward excuses?

Self-knowledge requires that a crude and pitiless light be cast equally on all aspects of our behavior. Excuses are cowardly, and incompatible with the nobility of a suprahuman aim.

For to transcend the human means to go beyond the limitations of the animal man, and excuses are simply the defense of our inferior nature, our Automaton. The Spiritual Witness sees no humiliation in acknowledging faults, for these weaknesses are obstacles to its control.

One must therefore take a definite stand, and either give in to the Automaton and excuse its vices, or else uncover without timidity every aspect of one's being, in order that the Spiritual Witness may regenerate the whole.

FIRST OBSTACLE: PERSONAL CONCERN

The struggle for control between the Ego and the Higher Self is like tightrope-walking, and indeed is a perpetual paradox. For one must learn to close one's own circuit and yet not limit oneself; one must be able to shut oneself in "the egg of cloud" and yet lose oneself in the illimitable.

One must in fact commit the supreme egoism of seeking one's own perfect realization, and do so with the supremely altruistic aim of learning to give oneself entirely.

The Tao says: "He alone can save others who has achieved his own salvation; but in saving himself he saves the world."

Chuang-tse says: "Only that which is fixed can fix that which is fixed."

But since the aim is the triumph of the Impersonal, the chief obstacle is anxiety for one's personal self.

The Personality defends its existence and prerogatives with ferocity. It is a gorgon, a dragon, and like Fafnir it resists and possesses.

It bears down with all its earthly weight on the vital flame which was entrusted to it at birth, and suffocates it, for fear that the fire, if it should flare up, would take control.

Its kingdom is that of contingency, whose many responsibilities every human being is obliged to accept.

It would be a mistake to try to apply to these practical values the same attitude as is needed toward the values of reality. On the contrary, they should be considered coldly as rational problems which can be solved in a mechanical way without the heart's becoming involved.

In this field we must not become identified with the object of our preoccupation, for then the gorgon would confuse all our values, cloud our judgment, and extract from us decisions in conformity with its merely personal interests.

Whether the problems concern material things or the conventions of social life, we must consider them apart from ourselves, and let the brain answer them by reducing them to their lowest terms, we ourselves remaining secure in the armor of indifference.

This is an opportunity to practice concentration of thought, the discernment which can discriminate between the requirements of a situation and the caprices of a Personality.

Obviously the thought of our ultimate aim should always be our criterion of judgment, but our emotional centers (the bile and spleen) must not be allowed to influence the decisions of our reason. Also the three lower activities—the physical, emotional, and mental—should be able to act independently of each other. The interference of one with another, sometimes going so far as inversion of function (of which we are not usually conscious), produces a chaos of thoughts and feelings whose interpretation is bound to be erroneous.

The confusion of these impulses with spiritual impulses is even more disastrous, for it creates not only false ideas of the origin of such impulses, but many psychic and physical disorders.

No valid path to the higher consciousness should cause or maintain a state of imbalance, physical, nervous, or mental. But this implies, of course, that one has at no point taken a wrong turning!

The false use of "identification" would be a wrong turning. One should try to identify oneself with everything that can bring Light and Wisdom, but to identify oneself with the vicissitudes of daily life would be an error;

they should be treated as external obligations to which the heart remains insensitive and impenetrable.

Training in this is the best way to develop a true sense of values, clarity of thought, and control of emotion.

Physical introspection, that is, preoccupation with health, is the other aspect of personal concern. It gives a tyrannical authority to the body, which takes advantage of this to attract attention to itself by creating any number of self-important pathological manifestations.

Anxiety for this mortal life deprives us of the power to transcend it and think of the immortal life. As the Gospel says, "He who would save his life shall lose it."

Wisdom offers a man control of his lower natures; but if he submits to being their slave, how can he ever attain it?

We have already studied the constitution of the human machine and how it should be kept in equilibrium. This is the first stage of self-knowledge, and brings its own reward. But we must not let the gorgon of selfishness divert the advantage to its own ends.

The body is the house made of clay and water; but it can become a magnet for the Spirit. And one would never guess how impetuously the Spirit rushes into a body which opens itself to receive it!

Everything comes to him who has the courage to lose himself in order to find the Universe.

The Abyss does not swallow him up; it is he who expands into the Abyss.

SECOND OBSTACLE: WRONG NOTION OF PROVIDENCE

If you wish to know the Divine Essence, do not give it an imaginary form.

If you wish to be aware of the Divine Driving-Force, do not invent it to fit your rules of logic and superficial morality.

If you wish to observe the predestination of things and beings, you must go back behind their successive avatars and comprehend the original act which brought them into being. In this original act you will find a Cause with inescapable consequences, which will proceed harmoniously or discordantly, according to how things follow their destined plan or become the victims of fortuitous circumstance.

That is the meaning of Providence.

A fertilized egg has in it the "providence"—that is, the plan of destiny—of the chicken which is to be hatched.

The Necessity, or Cause, which determined the creation of a nebula determines also the mode in which its substance shall develop; that is the "providence" of the nebula.

If you are unable to go so far back to the sources of Destiny, do not adopt, by way of lame explanation, the concept of an extracosmic God who, as general manager of the bourgeois world, hears the daily plaint of the good, gives each one his little reward, and punishes the wicked.

If the providence of such a God looked after the lives of all His creatures, would it not be responsible for the necessity which forces animals to kill each other for food? At that rate the goodness and pity which man has invented for God express themselves by giving life to some at the price of violent death for others!

This "providential" general manager would have to be held guilty of the most flagrant injustice and cruelty whenever the innocent suffer for the guilty, whenever children are tortured, crowds massacred, and villages wiped out by avalanche or volcano.

If you think it blasphemy to deny such an arbitrary "providence," take note that the blasphemy consists in confusing this all-too-human picture with the sublime gift of the Spirit, which by perpetual sacrifice gives life and sustenance to the universe, without discrimination, calculation, or selection.

That confusion, with its ignorance of causes, is responsible for the notion of God as pitiful or vengeful, of a Creator who doubts whether his works were opportune, and "repents Him" of having created them.

Let us be careful not to invent God in our own image! In the words of the Gospel, Divinity must only be worshipped "in Spirit and in Truth." So let us try to discover That Which Is, in truth.

First, before all and in all, there is the Absolute Principle, called by the Chinese sages Tao. This, according to the commentary of Chuang-tse:

> is the void center of the hub, the axis, the unnameable Principle, which has neither activity nor existence, properly speaking, but without which there is no reality and no truth; for It is the unqualified Potential, which, like a diffused light, illumines everything equally, giving each thing its true appearance.
>
> The Tao is the principle immanent in the spontaneity of the Universe, and it reveals itself by total indifference; it is "void" of prejudices, and makes no resistance to any free initiative. With It, the Unnameable, no individuation can be at odds.
>
> It gives life to the game, and yet remains outside the game; its one rule is nonintervention. It acts, in the sense of radiating tirelessly a sort of continuous vacuum. It provides a neutral milieu for the indefinite flux and reflux of spontaneous interactions.

We must next consider the Providence which each created thing carries within it.

This Providence is the innate element in it, and bears the consequences of its original cause.

The mistake is to try to bring in a God who would prevent causes from having consequences.

Various accidents, resulting from fortuitous secondary causes, can divert the working of the laws of Providence, and these may be regarded as karmic impulses, the source of discordances disturbing the primordial harmony, but no extracosmic Providence can intervene to prevent them.

Nevertheless human consciousness is capable of leaving these divergent paths to return to the way of Providence, the way of the One. This possibility is the meaning of Divine Compassion.

The perfect witness to Divine Compassion is the revelation of Christ, which offers humanity freedom from the divergences which have misled it from the plan of its destiny; for the way of the Christ is the way of unification, the human transmuted by the divine.

And if you still need a "divine brain" to look after and protect you, do not look for it in the Unknowable Power, but in those radiant beings called the Masters of Wisdom who illuminate the highest region of earthly life and are the intermediaries between humanity and the inaccessible Wisdom.

THIRD OBSTACLE: FALSE PITY

Of every form of genuine altruism there is a selfish imitation.

Compassion, which the Buddha preached, means that through consciousness of our mutual solidarity we have communion with the suffering of other beings. But only one who truly loves with the impersonal Love will be able, without a shade of selfish reflex, to join his heart to another's and so lighten suffering by effective compassion.

But suffering is not to be confused with pain. Pain is the result of a disorder, or of discord between personal inclination and the inclination of your providence.

Pain may be the result of karma or of present ignorance; but consciousness can find a way to avoid pain even when suffering is inevitable.

Pain is a reaction of the personality on either the physical or mental level.

But suffering is the struggle to take cognizance of a split between one's actual condition and the true condition that one may hope to attain, and the effort to return to health produces a state of tension.

If there is resistance on the personal level (physical or moral), the result is pain; but if the condition is consciously accepted, then pain can be eliminated and reduced to mere suffering, that is to say a trial; and one's vital reaction to the trial can even become a form of joy.

Suffering is the school of consciousness, which cannot be acquired without it.

Compassion consents to experience the trials of human suffering in order to better transmute them. It is an act of pure Love.

Pity is a personal reaction to the suffering of others as it appears to affect oneself. It is a reaction of fear that the same pain may come upon oneself, or else of condescension, the benefactor excusing himself for being privileged. In either case it is an impression related to one's personal sensibility and judgment rather than to its object.

Now, how can man, who knows so little, unravel the multiplicity of causes and effects? The Masters of compassion, who give up their beatitude to sympathize with human suffering, would not deprive anyone of the trials necessary to his evolution.

These words will offend those who are ''of this world'' and practice pity in order to be entitled to it themselves; that is why it is important to distinguish false charity and arbitrary pity from disinterested sympathetic altruism.

Nature has no pity; she follows the directions of ''providence'' for her Becoming. Each animal obeys the laws of its own kind, without pity for the prey on which its life depends. But apart from this there are many examples of altruistic behavior which in man might easily be attributed to pity. For example, female animals will nurse cubs which have lost their mother; a wounded creature will be fed and helped by its kind; an animal will risk its life for its young or for the herd. This type of altruism is obedience to a certain innate consciousness of animal solidarity. There is no calculation or judgment in it, and no pity, but there is justice in the sense of obedience to a law of the species.

Man, being the summit of the animal kingdom, is between this animal condition and the suprahuman condition in which all Nature's levels of consciousness are added together and one becomes conscious of all one's different consciousnesses.

Between these two extremes man's situation is uncertain, for his instinctive consciousness is obscured by his concrete mind, and his spiritual consciousness is usually hidden and undeveloped. This being so, the Automaton and its brain-consciousness exercise undisputed control, and it has the illusion of directing its acts and feelings with free will.

In actual fact, this free will amounts to no more than the possibility of obeying either the call of the suprahuman realm or else the law of human animality. He who obeys the former can rise to the suprahuman state; he who obeys the latter must follow the slow evolution of the animal man.

But in either case the two higher aspects of consciousness must not be suffocated by the Automaton, as they most frequently are. That is the third possibility, and then free will is an illusion, since the man merely obeys impulses, and these come not from his conscious Self, but from a personality manufactured by heredity, environment, education, custom, habit, and convention.

For each of these three possibilities there is a corresponding aspect of the feeling called pity.

The third case corresponds to spurious pity, which is a personal reflex either of reason or sensibility, more or less self-interested. This type of pity does not arise from either the instinctive or the spiritual consciousness.

There are two possible sources of altruism when it arises from a real feeling of solidarity with the sufferings of others. The first is the instinctive consciousness of solidarity in the species, either animal or human. This is the altruism of animals, or of a human creature which listens to its innate consciousness. The other source is the consciousness of the spiritual solidarity of Man; it belongs to that type of altruism which is totally free from egoism, the highest form of compassion, quite impersonal and disinterested. The Way of the Heart leads to it directly.

It does not follow from this that a man who cannot yet feel disinterested altruism must remain indifferent to the sufferings of others. Absence of altruism would be his ruin. But truly helpful altruism is incompatible with the selfish reflexes of pseudocharity, for the latter, being an illusion, prevents true compassion from being felt.

True compassionate altruism is the result not of an effort of will, but of the rending of the veil of virtue which prevents us from seeing our selfishness.

Tear that veil away, ignore your excuses, trample on your spurious pity, and let your own heart suffer the misery of others; then you will know how to relieve a suffering which you feel as if it were your own.

Men, animals, and all creatures living upon earth, are part of the Cosmic Man, whose states of consciousness they are. But man, since he is capable of reaching the highest state, should feel his solidarity both with those below him, whom he can help, and with those as yet above him, with whom he can collaborate.

For, whether he knows it or not, man cannot escape from this solidarity. He ought therefore to be wise enough to acknowledge it, since it lays upon him a responsibility.

The measure of this responsibility is that of your own consciousness. Enlarge therefore your consciousness by breaking the shell of selfish egoism. You will then be able to consider without danger the karmic consequences of every one of your acts, with no Divine ''pity'' to interfere with them. For when you feel your solidarity, and the responsibility it entails, you will understand that the law of karma cannot be used as an excuse to exempt you from the duty of altruism. Heaven shows you the example, in the Compassion which is immanent in the law of karma.

For in the world of Becoming, nothing is absolute. If one has lost the way, it is still and always possible to change direction and return to the Way foreseen by Providence in the beginning. This is the meaning of Divine Compassion.

But what motive can be strong enough to induce this change of direction?

There are three elements in the moral situation of any individual: first, the plan of his destiny, which was engraved upon the embryo; second, the deviations caused by education, lack of awareness, and the incoherence of the different aspects of the self, with the karmic complications which result therefrom; and third, the warnings of the spiritual consciousness which from time to time disturb us with anxiety or discontent.

These fugitive gleams of light are not strong enough to overcome our habits and the rational or passional resistances of the Personality. In consequence the Spiritual Witness is apt to manifest its presence by shocks or trials which for a moment or two startle the sleeper out of his dangerous unawareness. Whether these shocks are helpful or useless will depend on his reaction to them.

In such a case ignorant pity would prevent the trial and so destroy the increase of consciousness to which it might have led. Compassion, being more comprehensive, can help a man to transmute his suffering into realization of the light.

For relieving human misery, therefore, the most effective form of altruism is to become aware of our solidarity and of the help which this consciousness can give to others; for to show a light which helps to guide men out of the paths of confusion is to collaborate with the Divine Compassion.

But before one can show this light one must free oneself from the errors engendered by the illusion of pity.

If you wish to be generous, be generous, but it must be without judging either the suffering you relieve or the benefit you confer; it must be done without argument, without trying to impose your wishes, without trying to play the part of Destiny, whose plan you do not know.

If you want to help people, love them, and Love will tell you what to do.

FOURTH OBSTACLE: THE QUEST FOR SANCTITY

A saint, according to the canon of the Catholic church in its great days, is a man who practices to a heroic extent one of the three theological virtues.

The modern mind prefers to award halos to less compromising forms of sanctity. For in any human life the total realization of either Faith or Hope or Love would lead to such excesses as worldly wisdom could not approve—any more than it approved the absolute mysticism of St. Francis of Assisi.

Sanctity, according to our modern, more moderate criterion, is the prudent exercise of mediocre virtues, such as will keep us unspotted by the stain of sins recognized as such. What a pitiful creature such a saint would be, and how poor in knowledge of life!

But what enlargement of consciousness can one attain if one's experience of good and evil is limited to the observance or violation of imposed commandments?

To judge in this way is to prejudge; it is prejudice, not knowledge.

The most helpful way of acquiring consciousness is through the sense of one's own responsibility, the shock of a temptation overcome, and, if one fails, the precious burning sensation of remorse and shame.

This does not refer to the remorse that comes of being condemned by conventional or traditional moral standards, nor to obsession with the memory of a fault, which transforms a man into a guilty wretch through brooding over it. The remorse that liberates arises from a flash of Light illuminating the deeper motives of the fault. For this recognition to be wholly true one must be pitilessly neutral, and put aside any excuses suggested by the feeling or thinking of the Personality.

To redeem an error is to cancel out its evil effects, whether on others (which means making all possible reparation) or on oneself. The evil effect upon oneself is the violation of conscience, for this is a partial obliteration of consciousness. It can only be redeemed by a pitiless recognition of the impulses which lead to the offense, until the shame of it becomes so painful as to render any repetition of the act intolerable. That is the efficacious type of remorse, and destroys the roots of evil, provided that it continues to be felt until the result is totally achieved.

And it is the result which counts, not the time taken to achieve it.

Shame and remorse, when truly felt, have the sacrificial value of a purifying fire.

This type of remorse is of inestimable value as an initiation, and does not leave behind it any timid sadness or depressing regret, but a renewed ardor for the struggle; for the part of us that it touches is not our human vanity but our higher consciousness, and any shock which can awaken that is, for the wise man, a new contribution to fuller control and fuller Life.

Candidates for "irreproachable virtue" know nothing of this treasure, for their program is quite the contrary; they prefer to remain blind to their secret temptations, and hide their responsibility behind the authorities and their regulations.

Thus for the burning touch of experience they substitute security in obedience, and self-complacency for learning from one's mistakes.

Their obedience is a sleeping draught that puts their consciousness to sleep; for consciousness is only awake if every step on the path is receiving free, unconstrained, and deliberate examination.

He who rejects the experience which his soul requires, for fear of tarnishing his virtue, is in love with his earthly form and not with his eternal life.

Happy is he who has never, for fear of a burn or fall, extinguished this wonderful spark in himself or another; for that is the unpardonable sin. For, as the Gospel says, he that hath not put his talent to use shall be deprived of all that he hath.

The wise man tends the divine fire in himself until it overcomes all lesser fires. But a petty spirit prefers to conceal it behind false modesty and sacrifice it to the opinion of the world.

Poor earthbound man, so afraid of losing what he does not possess! For the integrity of his "purity" is simply the cloak with which his arbitrary judgment covers up his stifled instincts.

Poor man condemned to drag out endlessly a useless pilgrimage whose lessons he refuses to learn! He can drag on like that until the end of the world without finding the repose of Accomplishment, because he has sacrificed his God, which is his Fire of salvation, to the idol of his ego!

His fear of sin keeps him in the rut of mediocrity, where his longings are hypocritically disguised, fear atrophies his joy of life, and the reproaches of conscience are buried beneath a mountain of excuses.

Since he is justified in his own eyes, he has no further redemption to look forward to, and no hope of attaining the Kingdom of Heaven because he has created his own paradise on earth in the form of self-complacency.

If you stifle your passions, how can you recognize the force that is in you to be transmuted?

Idealistic dreams, the desires of the mind, are illusions without any substance, for there is nothing to be transmuted; only physical matter and earthly fire can be transmuted into Heavenly Fire. Mental impressions and projections are mere reflections; they can set in action the intellectual will, but not the vital fire that we have to awaken.

This fire reacts to instinctive forces only, be they in their animal or their spiritual aspect. The mutual reaction between these two poles, if controlled and directed consciously and wisely, will cause vitality and vital consciousness to awake and grow.

The petty persons of this world have called one of these poles Virtue and the other Vice. But the man who, in order to satisfy them, obeys the one and denies the other, will find himself suspended in the void. For, as in magnetism, to abolish one pole is to abolish both; it is the negation of life, the refusal of redemption for fear of committing a fault.

Any action by which you can transcend yourself and escape from your prison must of necessity be in some way excessive, for otherwise it would have no such power and would remain within the limits of the normal. But how will you ever dare to do anything brave if prudence keeps you locked up in the preoccupation of trying to avoid making a single mistake? It was not the unassailable Pharisee who becomes a friend of Jesus, but the sinner Zacchaeus, who recognized his unworthiness, and the prostitute from Magdala, whose love burned out the roots of her disgrace.

All this is only a strict and truthful observation of our own instinctive nature; it cannot be construed either as an encouragement to depravity or as a criticism directed at Christian "purity"; the scrupulous brahmin is meeting the same obstacle on the royal road, and so is the hermit who thinks of nothing but his own perfection.

Equally, he who seeks here a "mechanical" method for becoming a superman without a scratch on his virtuous door is narrow, and so low that to pass it one must be able, as the ancient Egyptians said, to "smell the earth." It is open only to those who have become simple, who have no pretension to be free of stain, but who open their hearts eagerly to the Light and in it forget their personal worries, fears, and prejudices.

FIFTH OBSTACLE: SENTIMENTALITY

Sentimentality is a spurious relationship created by the imagination between Nature and ourselves.

When a natural occurrence moves us, our emotion may be either genuine or spurious. It is genuine if it acts on our vital centers directly and spontaneously, without the intervention of imagination, egoism, or the spirit of possessiveness. It is spurious if sentimentality, which is egocentric, transposes it into the key of our likes and dislikes and imagines it relative to our personal impressions.

Man needs emotions, and when he cannot discover them in the domain of the real he creates them artificially inside his personality. But feelings concocted in this way are spurious because the relationships on which they are based have reference only to the Lower Self, which is never touched by anything except in a selfish manner.

The sentimental person judges all the reports of his senses by their concordance or discordance with his personal feelings and intellectual notions. He appreciates color only insofar as it charms himself; in music he likes only the tunes that reflect his own sentiments and recollections;

he likes satisfying harmonies, and finds discord irritating. In poetry he likes the seductive forms and conventional images which suit his personal idealism and sensuous feeling.

The sentimental person, in fact, lives in an artificial world of impressions and feelings which are only the reactions of his Automaton to anything which touches its emotions in a sensual, affectional, or intellectual way. And this emotional state is spurious, in the sense of "unreal," because it is the product of personal motives and not of contact with either natural or spiritual realities.

Sentimental emotion, since it affects only the mortal part of our being, does not in any way enlarge consciousness.

Animal instinct is closer to reality than this mental artifice by which ever-varying combinations of memory and emotion are used to play a kind of mental game.

The instinctive consciousness is quite different, for, provided that it is free from intellectual control, its function is to receive impressions from the elemental forces of Nature and to feel their influence acting upon us through our instincts. The accompanying emotion signifies the arousing of a sleeping awareness which transcends the mental concepts of the Automatic Self. This, however, becomes impossible if the intellect intervenes, doubting, selecting, refusing, rearranging, and "explaining" as shall suit its own arbitrary principles of interpretation.

For humanity the two real conditions are the two extremes, the physical and the spiritual. The two intermediary conditions—the astral or emotional, and the mental—are only temporary and relative, for their expressions can only be true when they correspond faithfully to the impressions received on the physical and spiritual planes. When the astral and mental play by themselves, or together, they simply create an entanglement of artificial feelings based on false impressions.

Sentimentality is a mirage and as unproductive as a desert. The traveler who believes in this mirage will pass his life in looking for the illusory oasis, and die of thirst a few paces from the well, not knowing which way to search.

Sentimentality apes love, but impersonal Love can burn it up as it burns up all destructible values, being itself the Living Fire that overcomes all powers both above and below.

SIXTH OBSTACLE: SATISFACTION

Happy the heart that cannot be satisfied! For he that is satisfied with the mediocre will never attain the great; and he whose cup can be filled with earthly things has not the capacity to hold heavenly things.

Physical life is a succession of petty satisfactions. The body is hungry, so it eats; sleepy, so it sleeps; desirous, so it claims possession.

For that which is created by separation requires to be satisfied with its complement; but every satisfaction contains within it the principle of a further separation.

This is the law that controls Nature, and it has an important consequence: Any desire which can be satisfied by an action on the physical, emotional, or mental plane belongs only to our mortal being. For all such satisfaction is a response to desire, pain, or remorse, and is thus a lowering of tension.

The sons of the earth fear excess of tension and wish to have it relieved by satisfaction. But the sons of Heaven seek tension, and refuse to relieve it with excuses, palliatives, or temporary pleasures.

The sons of Heaven are those human beings whose desire is for more than earthly joys. But this desire cannot become effective unless it can break out of the limits of its possible satisfactions. That which transcends them will be a sacrifice for the Automaton, which is part of Nature and indeed the crown of Nature, but only by breaking out of its limitations can we transcend it.

The Personal Consciousness, or Permanent Witness, if it can control the Automaton, can bring a human being up to the lower stage of the suprahuman realm, but it cannot attain the higher, which requires its regeneration by the Spiritual Self, so long as it is held down by the most dangerous form of satisfaction, which is self-satisfaction; for the Ego rejoicing in its own development is satisfied, and stuck, in its own selfish exaltation.

Happy therefore is the desire for the Absolute, which breaks the bounds of earthly desire and enlarges man's aspiration to complete expansion in the Universal Self.

SEVENTH OBSTACLE: ROUTINE

Routine is the rut in which our cells drag us atavistically along, chained lazily to our ancestors, with the secret aim of keeping us far off any new and liberating road.

Routine is the acceptance from other beings of loans which by force of habit we regard as our own.

In becoming attached to routine, say the Taoist sages, one loses one's own nature. One destroys one's true self if one becomes attached to other beings, for the Self should not be contaminated by others. One should rather take refuge in the To, the specific essence which is truly your own, for this is to take refuge in the Heavenly.

For the fully conscious man is his own aim, in virtue of his body which must be made to live; is his own road, in virtue of the Destiny immanent in his incarnation; is his own Heaven, in virtue of his incarnate soul.

PART FOUR

19

Reincarnation and Karma

The first question that the curious ask about the wisdom tradition is almost always: "What becomes of us after death? Are we born again? When, how, and how often?"

But only too commonly the spirit in which the question is asked invites an absurd answer. It is as if one should ask a pious Roman Catholic of what material the apostles' heavenly thrones are made.

Yet that is not just a joke; some deeply religious people would examine the question seriously, and each would find an answer in his imagination. For once the invisible world is under discussion, any theory will .be listened to—"One guess is as good as another, isn't it?"—and one can safely make assertions which no one will come from Beyond to contradict.

It seems to be the same with reincarnation; the ignorant can defend their opinions easily enough! Unfortunately neither their opinions nor their religious beliefs will prevent them from enduring after death the inevitable consequences of their karma, which one might call the law of their own necessity.

All religions taught reincarnation until Christianity came and publicized the principle of redemption, which can, in the man in whom it is realized, bring reincarnations to an end.

Now, the Christ also taught Nicodemus that no one can enter the Kingdom of Heaven unless he be born again, and, more precisely, unless he "be born of water and of the spirit.... That which is born of the flesh is flesh; and that which is born of the Spirit is spirit" (John 3:5-6).

In other words, the divine life of the Kingdom of Heaven can only be enjoyed by the immortal being whose spiritual seed (the Spiritual Witness) has regenerated the Ego-Consciousness (the Permanent Witness), which is its medium of expression. And "medium" here implies also the mean between high and low, between spiritual and physical, as water lies between air and earth.

This is the rebirth which the last purifying reincarnation makes possible, before or even after death.

By this rebirth a human being becomes a Son of Man; for "no man hath ascended up to heaven, but he that came down from heaven"—that is, from his own spiritual being—"even the Son of man which is in heaven" (John 3:13)—that is, in the divine state. And of this the Christ is the prototype, the human made immortal and united with the Divine, which has regenerated it.

Some modern writers, in spite of the teaching of many centuries, deny reincarnation except in rare cases. But if one asks the present teachers of the tradition, they will reply as we do here: "If I denied reincarnation I should be lying, but if I assert it without explaining its real meaning, you would imagine things which are not so."

Mere common sense obliges us therefore, before penetrating more deeply into the subject, to examine the questioner's depth of understanding. What does he know of his spiritual state? What knowledge of it can his brain-consciousness offer him? What does he know of his metaphysical being? Or his astral nature? Has he developed his intuitive faculties?

If he has no experience of these different domains, if he cannot even reanimate his physical body at will, how can he understand the various possibilities of reincarnation?

Most people, if one speaks of the physical world as a mere transitory appearance, are scandalized, yet they refuse to train the faculties which would give them access to the invisible realm. What language, then, could one use to explain to the popular mind postmortem conditions with which it can make no contact? One might as well talk of color to a man born blind.

Surely it is obvious that your convictions, when devoid of any check, are founded upon your preferences, and are of no more value than the opinions of armchair strategists discussing the plans of a battle without any information about the troops engaged.

Basically, you are anxious for the survival of your personal self, by which you mean your acquired framework of brain-knowledge, your scientific, social, or aesthetic ideals, your ambitions, in fact the little world so laboriously built up around your Ego, whose loss would seem to you a cosmic disaster. How disillusioned you would be if you would let your higher consciousness tell you that this artificial Ego is just the unnecessary luggage which the individual jettisons after death!

Few men can accept this reality and not revolt—as if their denial of it could impede the working of a cosmic law!

But illusion so thoroughly blinds men that they would be willing to lose a limb, and then another limb, and even one of their intellectual faculties, provided that they could keep in a future world the notions and appearances which have constituted on earth their social, intellectual, and emotional personality.

But, among all your attachments, preferences, and varying opinions, have you so much as selected those which you will ask death to perpetuate as your true eternal self? Do be careful to avoid a choice in questionable taste! Where the time is so long, that would be sickening!

The purpose of this irony is to help your real self to prevail against the selfish routines of your unseeing personality. If this chapter revolts you, postpone reading it until you are more inclined. But if your will is toward the Light, observe what follows.

If you want to know why and how reincarnation happens, let us make an experiment. Lie down, and see that the body, and above all the nerves, are completely relaxed. Then repeat, slowly and with attention, these words, trying as you do so to convince yourself that they are entirely true: "I abandon here and now all worry, all preoccupations, all personal will....I wash away all grief and all regret, all spite and vengeance....I give up all personal love, all plans, all longings, and all hopes for earthly things."

If you try really to be sincere in making these assertions, I defy you to speak the words without misgiving. Certain flame-hot fibers will revolt in you, will refuse such a surrender and contradict any such undertaking. Those are the threads that will drag you back to earth. Inevitably!

Spiritual states have nothing in common with your memories, or with the imaginings and intellectual interests of your earthly being; but those memories impress their emotional attraction upon your Ego-Consciousness, and this prevents its liberation and causes you to return to earthly existence, by attraction, by the yearning for completeness. This is one of the most important aspects of the law of karma.

We are obliged to use the Sanskrit word *karma* because there is no exact correspondence in our European languages. One can say, however, that karma is the true meaning of Necessity.

Karma is the inevitable succession of effects resulting from the deeds, words, and actions of human life.

If you shout toward an echoing cliff, you cannot stop the reverberation of the repeated sound. So too will each one of your acts bear its consequences, and you will have to undergo their effects until they are completely exhausted.

The first incarnation of your *ka* determined the time and manner of your first earthly existence, and its conditions regarding parents, place, and so forth. The time, manner, and conditions became in turn the causes of very many effects, that is, of influences modifying the secondary characteristics and behavior of your Ego. These were then able to complicate and sometimes upset the rhythm of action which the plan of your destiny had designed for you. Thus do new causes produce new consequences, and so reincarnation remains inevitable until the effects of these disturbances have been canceled out.

Thus are formed the links in your chain of karma. With some acts, several incarnations may be necessary before their repercussions are finally exhausted. An insult or a murder may lead its perpetrator to reincarnate at a place and time which will give him an opportunity for reparation; but in this there is no deliberate choice, no design of punishment, only Necessity, the inevitable play of reactions arising from the crime.

If the hatred provoked by an act of violence is expressed in vengeance, then the vengeance will arouse more hatred followed by further vengeance, as in the custom of the vendetta, and this will postpone indefinitely the exhaustion of the evil karma.

A race, like an individual, has its karma, or necessity. But we must distinguish between karma and destiny.

If you strike the note C, it sets in vibration certain other notes which are known as its harmonics. One hears the fundamental C, the C an octave higher, G a fifth higher still, the second octave C, with the mediant E above it, and even further harmonics determined by numerical law but too faint to be distinguished. All these harmonics are the destiny of the original C.

If the string is damaged or badly played on, a wrong sound will be produced, and will continue to be heard until its vibrations are exhausted. This is an example of karma, or necessity turned aside from the plan of destiny.

But, you will say, what about free will? If I am brought to earth by previous impulses, and all my acts are determined in a succession that I cannot escape, then my decisions are being dictated to me by fate, and I am just an irresponsible marionette.

To a superficial observer of this intricate drama, the objection may be valid. Let us, however, note the finer points of the tragicomedy.

The scene is a familiar one, determined by the need to have certain experiences or to pay certain karmic debts. But the atmosphere is heavy with storm.

Various people move about in the background, some brought by karma, like yourself, some led by their destiny, and others attracted by the impending drama.

In the foreground, yourself, the hero of the story. Let us have a look at you through our many-dimensional binoculars, which will reveal the complex movements of all your states of consciousness, as well as the urges arising in your Automaton.

First I see a universe of organs and canals arranged about two poles and central sun. Liquid and fluid streams of energy flow constantly to and fro around the organic centers. Some of these act in combination, others struggle to prevail against each other. I see how lymphatic weakness, the unresponsiveness of spleen or hypochondria, and the bitter reactions of the bile make their effect upon the will and consume the vital energies.

Looking more closely, I see each organ influenced by the planet with which it holds analogy, attracting and repelling various substances according to its affinities, and, like the planets, creating around it a sphere of influence not static, for an organ's working modifies the humors just as the movement of the planets alters the balance of the heavens.

Suddenly trouble arises; a critical case must be decided immediately, and contradictory interests are involved. The ensuing anxiety creates a disturbance of the bile, and sets off a chain reaction in the intellect and emotions, whereby all the data of the problem become confused.

Such a moment might be called an ''astrological crisis''; it seems a trap from which the actor cannot escape. What will he decide to do?

He is so tense, as a result of this internal disorder, that he fails to notice the various minor actors on the scene—some ''good intentions'' in the foreground, an ancient spite coming in, ambitions elbowing their way to the front, and all of them making eddies in the currents that influence him.

Yet the poor man imagines himself alone, as he struggles with his uncertainty.

But watch! Something has touched his spiritual mainspring, and from the depths of his substance a vague awareness wakens, a light comes into the hero's eyes, and from heaven, as if by chance, comes a flash, revealing an unforeseen solution.

Then from some deep dungeon rises an old habit of mind, with its pretorian guard of rigid principles, and their gaunt shapes block the newly seen opening of the path. The actor searches for it in desperation, but the moment of Light has passed, and darkness conspires to thwart him.

However feeble the voice of conscience, still it makes his heart contract. The contest seems unequal, and he hesitates to break the resistance down by violence. What should he do?

He looks to us, so let us give him an answer.

''Poor marionette, do at least look at the forces that are playing with you, before you take a decision!

''All the present constituents of your being are agglomerations of previous experiences which hide your real Self, and all are trying to live their own lives, taking advantage of your ignorance. You are a kingdom in anarchy, waiting for its master to wake and organize it. Do you find that hard to believe?"

"What can I do? I am only an Automaton without free will; all my actions are predetermined!"

"There you are wrong! For even if your acts are determined by outside influences, and by your karma, nevertheless you have at every critical moment liberty not to will them, or rather, liberty not to oppose the destiny which was impressed upon you at birth. For that destiny is your true harmony.

"You have the choice between this not-willing, and a free decision to will something different—which means to create disharmony.

"So your famous free will looks rather negative; you do not need an effort of will when you follow the impulse of harmony with your true being."

"On the contrary, it takes an enormous effort of will to restrain my evil instincts!"

"That is because you do your fighting with arguments. You are using the wrong weapons. The heart's appeal might be heard, but you are using the brain instead. Men decide their differences by memory and reason, which plead too coldly to gain the final verdict. Rational thinking does not hold the keys of the Kingdom of Heaven, for the keys are Simplicity, Faith—which is identification—and Love—which is communion with the Fire.

"If you think as the world thinks, your so-called faith is not an experience impressed upon your consciousness; it is founded either on argument or on acceptance of current beliefs.

"Your charity, too, is only conscience money, or perhaps an insurance policy for the life beyond.

"And your morality is equalitarian, ignoring the spiritual needs of individuals. Its legal schedule stifles the inner voice of conscience which tells you the requirements of harmony from moment to moment, and suggests appropriate action. Most frequently this action is submission to the events by which it gathers experience."

"That's fatalism!"

"Not at all; it is agreement with the urge to attain harmony with the plan of your destiny. The inward ear, if it is trained, can pick up warning of material and spiritual dangers, just as simple, instinctive people do who do not cultivate divergency of the will."

"But how can one distinguish the urge to harmony from the divergency of the will?"

"That is the crucial point; one learns from the idea of karma. A man who by a process of reasoning chooses what he believes to be his good may be mistaken, for a given action may be required of him by the plan of his destiny.* But if he is convinced of an unescapable necessity, he will instinctively avoid any act that would aggravate his karma. With further development he can learn to counteract the kinetic energy of the karmic wheel, and instead of being a marionette he becomes a master."

The scene has altered a little; there is a rift in the clouds, and the actor has the courage to turn around and look at his companions. As he observes them, they slowly withdraw to the background, returning to their proper stations. Force of habit has grown weaker, yet still it returns, threatening to obscure the way. Evening is coming on. Will the hero be able to take advantage of the clearance, or will he again let his free will mislead him?

Thus the curtain falls on a scene in which you, as seeker, have been both actor and spectator. Being a matter of life and death, it is a tragedy; but it is also a comedy, since ignorance makes human effort so frequently absurd. When the scene is over, the actors will consider the impression it has produced; and perhaps some of them will not appear again.

The actors will continue to appear until the kinetic energy of the wheel of karma is finally exhausted.

It is the thirst for satisfaction that draws human beings back to the places where they have loved and suffered and vibrated, as it brings back the criminal to the scene of his crime.

Karmic necessity makes the perfect foundation for the moral law, philosophically speaking; but if applied exclusively, it would seem cruel.

In itself, karma requires that one should have respect for everything that happens to oneself or others, this being logically regarded as the necessary consequence of previous actions requiring justice and reparation.

An equally logical consequence would be an attitude of impassive indifference to the misfortunes or misery of one's neighbor.

I can hope to diminish the impact on my neighbor of effects that I have caused, but not of effects which he has set in motion himself.

If I see a human being suffering, and I can help him, that will not modify the karmic consequences of his acts, but I shall perhaps be able to reduce his resentment, improve his rhythm, and thus prevent him from making his burden heavier.

We must not forget that we are all members of the Cosmic Man, and this solidarity means that, to a certain extent, we participate in all that affects others. To that extent, therefore, we can improve their state of

*See Chapter 18, second obstacle.

being by the essential reality of our own. This is how the influence of impersonal love can be effective in compensating the harshness of the law of karma.

If the final aim and liberation of a spiritual being is to cease returning to terrestrial existence, it is desirable nonetheless that reincarnation should continue until the bonds of karma have been dissolved and the various aspects of consciousness united.

It is difficult to explain schematically what is or is not possible, but we can aid our imagination with the analogy of a crystal.

The specific axial system of a given crystalline form may be taken to represent the Divine *Ka*. And as a crystal dissolves in water, its formative solution represents its medium of expression.

If a very small crystal of the same substance is added to a sufficiently concentrated solution, identical crystals will be formed; in other words, the substance of the medium will be induced to reconstitute itself in accordance with the principles of its *Ka*; this represents reincarnation.

But if the solution is insufficiently concentrated, then the crystal dropped in will simply dissolve into the water and remain in a state of nonexistence; that is, it will not be able to reincarnate.

Though the analogy is not perfect, it helps us to understand the condition of discarnate beings, that is, of their Ego-Consciousness or Intermediate *Ka*. Some of them, not having created any homogeneous medium, cannot crystallize out around their Divine *Ka*, nor yet take form in reincarnation for lack of any center of attraction. Like the crystal dissolved in a foreign or too-dilute solution, they are in danger of remaining after death in that state of latency which is known to the West as Limbo—unable to make themselves real in either the one state or the other.

It was to escape this danger that the ancient peoples used so often the indirect means of portrait statues of the deceased, pictures of him enjoying his favorite occupations, Tablets of Ancestors, and so forth; the purpose of these was to act as a terrestrial bait, by reason of the emotional attraction which they can exercise so long as the Ego-Consciousness possesses an astral body.

To understand what really happens in reincarnation one must first know the elements of the human constitution.

That which reincarnates is that which cannot be destroyed by death; that is, the two aspects of consciousness, the Spiritual Witness and the Permanent Witness, also called the Divine *Ka* and the Intermediate *Ka*.

If during its life on earth the Permanent Witness has integrated into itself the animal consciousness of its body (its animal *Ka*), it has thus created the medium in which its "glorious body" will be able by degrees to build itself up through communion with the Spiritual Witness—until, whether before or after death, both are united and so attain their final liberation.

But until this final victory is achieved, there is always a danger that the Spiritual Witness will withdraw if during life on earth the Personality refuses to obey it.

And whatever powers the Permanent Witness may have acquired, if death catches it in this state of dissociation from its higher self, it will only be able to follow in the other world the same selfish dispositions as it evinced on earth. It is always the unquenchable thirst of the Ego, wanting its own way, that prevents the possibility of union with the Divine *Ka,* the Spiritiual Witness to the Impersonal Self, whose power it perceives and envies.

This is why the funerary pictures of ancient Egypt represent man as "in search of his *Ka,*" without which he cannot attain his final immortality.

This anxious search for the Divine *Ka* corresponds to the pains of damnation by which Christian theology expresses the sufferings of the damned as a consciousness of being deprived of God, who has become inaccessible to them.

Both descriptions correspond to the same reality, except for the question of perpetuity; for the funerary scenes of Egypt represent the obstacles which prevent the discarnate person from being united with his *Ka,* but do not present them as an irremediable conditon of perpetual hell.

This state of unsatisfaction may also lead to a reincarnation under such conditions as will increase the inflation of the Ego, especially if it has acquired in its previous life the first key* to the suprahuman realm, namely control of its three lower states of being which are part of Nature.

This explains the innate disposition which certain persons have toward a real mastery of human life, but which they use for the very opposite of spiritual realization, namely temporal domination.

If for this reason, or by any other denial of the light, a man renders himself incapable of regeneration by his Spiritual Witness, it may happen that the latter will withdraw completely and finally, thus exposing the conscious "I" to that dissolution of which theologians speak with horror as "the second death."

Whatever be the cause and conditions of such a withdrawal, which may occur either during or after life on earth, a man thus emptied of his immortal elements is reduced to the condition of a human animal which

*See Chapter 6.

can no longer enter into the suprahuman realm. After his death his animal souls, or Inferior *Kas,* will try to take form in their own realms, animal, vegetable, or mineral, and thus restart the cycle; and in the course of it there is a chance of their being once again ensouled by Spirit.

Thus the divine compassion is still at work.

This too may explain such strange doctrines as metempsychosis, provided we consider it the incarnation of residue.

20

The Masters

Tradition asserts the existence of certain Masters of Widsom; but this needs to be clarified. Among other things, it has been said that there are three Masters as guides on the three great mystic paths—the Master of Knowledge, the Master of Love, and the Master of Action.

First we must understand the meaning of the three paths. They are the three ways in which enlargement of consciousness is possible.

Knowledge comes from an enlargement of consciousness by which the mind is identified with the thing known. Its criteria and characteristics have already been described, and it does not in principle comprise any form of action.

Love means complete giving, in the sense of an unlimited expansion of "Myself" into the Universal Self. It wants nothing but to radiate, and acts always impersonally, giving without discrimination, for there is no personal will. This expansiveness leads again to identification; but it may not express itself in any intelligible knowledge.

Action, in principle, is movement, the execution of a will; for without will there is no action, and will itself is a movement toward a definite aim. Thus will and movement have much in common.

Mystically, action is the execution either of a will that must be obeyed or of an impulse due to necessity of circumstances. But the necessity is always ultimately the effect of an earlier personal act of will, sometimes long ago, the consequences of which have produced this obligation to further action. In other words, all action is obedience to a will.

But action does not include knowledge, for knowledge is obscured by both movement and will. For this reason guides and instructors must limit themselves to the very minimum needed for the discharge of their mission.

The man of action should first examine the quality of the will which he obeys; for the property of action is action for its own sake, in complete acceptance of the directions given, and without care for the consequences.

But in any case it is wiser not to divide the mystical quest into three such definite categories; it may help beginners, but hardly corresponds with reality. No element in life can be dissected like a corpse. Everything living is complex, and each of the three ways should be regarded as a strong tendency which can only realize itself by being to some extent combined with one or both of the others.

We can now return to our original question. Are there Masters with suprahuman powers who watch, judge, and help us? If so, where do they live, and who are they?

If we try to explain this by using the technical language of existing doctrines, we shall run into a dispute about the meanings of words. It would be better to examine the facts in a new spirit, trying to forget our preconceived ideas and terms.

If we cast an impartial glance over the human groups inhabiting our earth, we can gather a rich harvest of symbols, dogmas, and cults, besides finding the most curious practices, the most contradictory codes of morals, and the most uncompromising fanaticisms. On Good Friday the different communions of the One True Faith fight in the Church of the Holy Sepulchre. In the jungles of Africa fetishes keep alive the primitive doctrine of animism. Next to the Buddhist disciples of compassion we find Kali's ferocious Thugs; for both Shiite and Sunnite the muezzin chants the oneness of Allah; and Zoroaster's Parsees assert the duality of the First Principle!

And yet from every breast rises the anxious cry: "Help us, protect us, give to us, O you gods, angels, saints, marabouts, djinns! Do for us what we have not the courage to do for ourselves!"

How pathetic is humanity, always talking of independence and liberty, and yet unable to regain its original title, Lord of Creation. Adam, the Red Earth Man, could "name" all the other creatures, which means that he had within him the power to master them. O man, what have you done with your power?

The trouble comes, perhaps, from that strange legend which every sect of every faith whispers secretly to itself: "Our own Messiah is coming! Our King of the World is nigh! The Mahdi is ours! The Christ is ours! Our Master will come and reign over all nations!"

From East to West, all fanatics hang on to this hope, and every cult's believers make it their own. All are waiting, praying, calling on Him Who shall bring them—what? Light? Alas, no! World dominion, of all things! In their obsession with temporal power, that is how priests and people have translated the great promise of the Gospel concerning the Master:

"Watch therefore; for ye know not what hour your Lord doth come" (Matthew 24:42)—a passage referring to the new influx and awakening of the Divine Man in those who are so disposed.

But who is the Master?

Have patience. You want to know too soon; he who would win perfect knowledge must begin by recognizing his perfect ignorance. If you were not deceived by words, you would not have failed to recognize the Master already.

Have you never, in silence, reflected on the deep meaning of this idea, or felt the shiver of his actual presence?

The Master is that power which in a moment of unbalance seizes you, overcomes you, reveals you to yourself, sometimes even, by surprise, succeeds in making you the king of yourself.

The Master is the speaker's thrilling point of argument, which suddenly moves you; the metalworker's skill, when the perfection of his "appropriate gesture" grips you; the unexpected reaction of a chemical combination, showing an unknown law at work against previous calculation.

He is the beggar who disturbs your ease by appearing, famished, on the doorstep of the restaurant where you are having a good dinner. He is the sea, first peaceful, then seizing the fisherman with terror, as its great waves unfurl the tempest and dismast the ship, unless the man has been able to catch the wild rhythm of the elements and trim his sails at the favorable moment.

He is the longing to kill which bursts forth in a jealous man who thought himself certain of his virtue.

But how can the Master be such moments of violence?

He can, for if there is a good Master there is also a bad one. The "Master" is the forced identification with one's inner being, when one is seized by an irresistible vibration which puts one into unison with it. For at such a moment that vibration is your master. One can only master that which one knows, and one does not know this impetuous power—or at least one has failed for a moment to recognize it, and so one is taken by surprise, and identified and confounded by it. That is "the visit of the Master."

Human masterhood, on the other hand, is continuous awareness, so steady that it can no longer be taken by surprise.

Such moments, however they come, are moments of blessing, for they are opportunities for Light, which would transfigure you if you knew....

Men are afraid of them, of course. They prefer to remain in ignorance of their impulses of cruelty and hatred, hiding them in some dark corner of their substance, whence one day they will spring out uncontrollably. But if one looks them in the face, lets them vibrate in consciousness, they reveal certain secret tendrils which are growing without one's knowledge. And once they are known, one can learn to destroy them.

We are afraid of emotion. If your heart bleeds for the hungry beggar, you will not enjoy your meal. And we think it safer to distrust the emotional power of words; it might be disturbing if we allowed them too much importance. So let us be careful! Let us be afraid of life! Let us not see the Light "by mistake"!

How happy is the simple heart, which, without respect of persons, can salute the Master at his passing, whatever face he shows: thunderbolt, shame or terror, enthusiasm or lust, beggar or genius, Machiavelli or Jesus. That which wakes the Spirit in you is an appeal from the Master of your soul.

It comes in many ways—desire, remorse, the longing for excess or for infinity, the creative urge—but it is always a flaming up of the Fire that was buried in you the day that you were "given" a living soul, and from time to time it melts you and you become a volcano.

We often speak of the soul, but we do not speak of this Fire.

The soul of imperfect man is complex, so much so that its anarchic elements can set in motion urges which have no apparent connection, and one ceases to recognize oneself.

But though its manifestations are various, there is only one Fire in the world.

The Original Fire is one and indivisible; but when it has descended into a substance and incubated there, it divides into two opposing fires.

There are then two poles—the accepted world and its black shadow, or celestial fire and terrestrial fire, desire and will. There is therefore conflict, and out of this conflict come suffering, uncertainty, and sickness.

Where there is conflict there is life, and if the fires of the two poles meet for an instant there is a flash. Thus every conjunction means the momentary destruction of a form; but since terrestrial nature cannot ever remain static, the decomposition of any part creates new life and activity. This is a key which, with profound meditation, will open many doors.

The Fire is always Fire; it remains, but it transforms everything. Hidden in the seed which the wet earth will awaken, it may slumber long before its resurrection. But when it does awake, it gently warms into life, and begins to show its activity by dividing into two principles, so that conflict arises. "Its revolution creates the movement of life."

Here let us make a pause; for we are on the edge of a mystery so profound that there must first be a dialogue between heart and reason:

"This is inconceivable! How can That, the Spiritual Fire, which is the living motive-power of everything, be a long time awaiting its resurrection? Why this patience? Can the principle of life be inertia? It gives us our will to live, and has it none of its own? Does That which is Reality not try to overcome the illusions of form? Does That which is Truth have no will to prevail over discord?''

"You, O brain, think thus because you always analyze and compare; you judge the world by yourself. But in Nature there is no good or evil, only attraction and repulsion. Those are the forces which the essential Fire obeys, and they are elementary, not rational.''

"What! Is the Spirit not its own master?''

"No. Once caught in the net of matter, it must obey the necessities of the realm in which it is incarnate, just as the ovum, once fertilized by the sperm, must infallibly follow through the phases of gestation of its species.''

"So it is a prisoner in its own substance?''

"Yes, until the union is dissolved; then it is delivered from its bonds, and can resume life by uniting with whatever in that substance has developed an affinity with it.''

"But this could only happen by means of death.''

"It is a death which happens innumerable times in your life, every time a piece of matter becomes your own living flesh.''

"What do you call that which is bound like this?''

"The sensitive soul.''

"What! Is the soul made of matter?''

"No, but it appears to be because it always requires a substance as its vehicle.''

So, though the Spiritual Principle is simple, this soul we are talking of is complex, because it is the agglomeration of all the vital tendencies which have, so to speak, been magnetically patterned around the original ''spiritual nucleus'' (the chromosome, as it were) in the course of its peregrinations through material existence. This complex soul—to give it an exact name—was called in Egypt the *Ka,* and its different aspects will be described later.*

Each aspect of the *Ka* strives to assert itself, and tries to monopolize the will to its own advantage. Only by becoming conscious of the interplay of these diverse elements can one realize oneself as a complete and harmonious individual.

That is the aim of human existence.

It is an absolute necessity for every individual life before returning to its divine source to attain total consciousness of the matter in which it is incarnate; for that which has once departed from Unity cannot find eternal life without this resurrection, that is, without total realization.

"And what about that which has not departed?''

*See Appendix II.

"There we enter upon the world of Archetypes, of which all terrestrial creatures are symbols."

Before being skeptical, consider this: Why is it incredible that a harmony of archetypal powers should constitute a spiritual world which with its energies interpenetrates and controls our material world, when we see in the nerve-centers of that microworld, the brain, a focus of energy which controls all the physical and mental functions of the physical body? There is, however, this difference: that what in the one is divisible, and an effect, in the other is indivisible, and a cause.

Herein resides the mystery of the spiritual hierarchies which can exist in the heart of Unity without losing their own being. To imagine this is not merely difficult, but impossible. We can only conceive it by the communion of that in us which is of the same nature as our indestructible Origin. To our minds, which cannot understand without making comparisons, that is to say oppositions, this diversity in Unity is intolerable.

Light, however, can provide us with a simile, for it is white in itself, and only shows the seven colors when it is broken by a prism.

Light is a vibration of the essential Fire, and the Fire is a manifestation of the original Word.

The Word is That which has incarnated, and That which has incarnated is, according to Plato, "the Same."

"The Same" is identical with "That," and in spite of its incarnations "That" has never been divided.

In every incarnation all the essential Numbers are incarnated in a single Fire.* They will become manifest successively in the "becoming" of the forms, but they are virtually simultaneous.

"That" takes form in the different realms of earthly life, and in each of its forms it increases the perfection of its consciousness.

Here we reach at last the world of the true "Masters." When a man on earth has succeeded in incarnating his divine *Ka* and achieved total conscience, he has realized his "glorious body," his indestructible being, for which death is only a liberation from physical obstacles.

He can then live in whatever country or "spiritual milieu" suits him, or remain accessible to humanity in order to help its evolution, or choose a further incarnation in order to fulfill his task of helping.

Such, in their different conditions, are the "Perfect Men" who may be called the Masters.

Nothing in this is contrary to common sense, only the fantastic imaginings which have been built up around it are misleading. For we should never forget that between the spiritual world and the physical world

*The Kabalistic Kether. (Trans. note)

there is a gulf as impassible for our cerebral faculties as a brick wall is for our physical body.

Every human thought, therefore, is fallible, unless it can restrict itself to expressing faithfully that which "identification" has revealed to it.

And further, from the Light of the Sages, whether inspired by a Master or rediscovered in himself (for it comes to the same thing), every teacher will catch that ray which matches the "color" of his own soul.

The light that the sun casts on the planets is the same for all, but each planet reflects it according to its own color, and the radiation that it returns is determined by its constitution. In this inevitable diversity of color there is no treachery or false transmission, but it does explain why no teacher, however great, can call himself the sole possessor of the Truth. He can only teach according to the type and "color" of his own soul, and to his capacity for faithful representation. Beyond this limit he would be exceeding or misdirecting his mission, and adding a heavy responsibility to his burden of karma.

For his disciples, however, the temptation to high claims is all the greater because they do not know the limits of their Master's mission and often enlarge it, through either vanity or unperceptiveness. This is a real danger, which all the illuminated must guard against by preserving a selfless and impersonal attitude.

Every type of teaching naturally attracts the disciples whom it suits. No disciple should ever forget what the Master knows quite well: that Wisdom is not to be found by all men, however well disposed, along the same road and under the same aspect. This has been very loyally understood and practiced by the sages of Tibet, who sometimes direct their pupils to a different master whose teaching will be more suitable for them than their own.

Disciples too should practice the same wisdom, and never, by a shameful sectarian jealousy, prevent the awakening of the Light in others.

21

The Elite

In attempting to throw light on some of the problems which cause anxiety to modern man, one must first decide to whom to address oneself. What with professional prejudice and educational bias, there are so many differences of culture and belief, such multiplicity of opinions and such divergent lines of approach, that it seems hard to find any common language.

Aside from the great mass whose interests are limited to material cares and personal ambitions, many people today are troubled by a thirst for knowledge concerning the essential problems of life, or by the fact that their deepest aspirations remain unsatisfied. Both these anxieties are the result of uncertainty; the way is uncertain because the goal is uncertain. In either case the solution would seem to lie in knowledge of the laws which condition life on earth and define its aim. The danger is that any such teaching would be taken for dogma, and have its advocates and opponents, unless of course one could provide the proof of it. But the proof can only be found by individual experience.

One is tempted, therefore, to offer the answer to an elite only. But how is the elite to be selected?

An elite is always selected in relation to an aim. If your aim is the control of nations, then your elite will consist of military and economic magnates, and the directors of political policy. If the aim is to create a racial aristocracy, then the members will be chosen for their physical and intellectual prowess. If the aim is to attain the highest destiny of humanity, then the elite will be selected for the qualities required by that aim. This highest destiny has been exemplified in history by the appearance from time to time in different races and civilizations of certain great ones who have attained the highest point of human development. Their achievement may be regarded as fabulous, or godlike, yet why did they appear to offer us the example of a suprahuman kingdom, or condition as a possible aim?

We think so much of progress in the sciences, of the wonderful power of mathematical thought, of discoveries in machinery and biology, that we have lost sight of the only kind of progress which is of value for the essential aim of man, namely the proof that his existence is eternal, that his development continues even after the death of the body, and that he possessses faculties which enable him to discover spiritual reality and discern the relationship of the realities of the senses to this higher reality.

His power of thought may fill the intellectual man with pride, and cloud the vision of his true destiny; but reality will take its revenge when some fortuitous development makes nonsense of the most artful deductions of professors, politicians, and psychologists. And its last revenge is taken at the moment of death, when the dying man, forced to abandon everything he has lived for, may well ask what he has profited by it all. Whether or not believing in survival, a man does feel the need for some continuation to justify his struggles and atone for his disappointments. But the belief in an afterlife—which can begin in this very existence by the attainment in some slight degree of that transcendent state which the sages have called ''the realm of the suprahuman''—this belief is often rejected only out of a false timidity. Man would sooner die in the dreary belief of having wasted one's life, than encounter the superior smile of the skeptic!

Others have been attracted by techniques for acquiring what are called magical or psychic powers, which produce abnormal phenomena in the lower levels of life or matter, abnormal physical, emotional, or mental states: but in this there is nothing of the suprahuman.

The suprahuman realm is a state in which spiritual awareness predominates over psychological awareness of the lower levels, and where the universal prevails over the particular. The sages who speak of it condemn as serious obstacles the multiplicity of desires and complicated notions. They do not speak of magical powers, but of the inherent abilities of the spirit when controlling matter. And they do not speak of willpower as a means to produce phenomena, but of the absence of violence, egotism, and hatred; for without these our human and animal aggressiveness would no longer be dangerous.

Each in his own language speaks of those elect beings who have acquired the qualities needed for entering on the suprahuman realm (those who have been ''called'') and those who have actually attained it (the ''elect'').

Whether we study the Gospels, or Lao-tse, or the Egyptian Masters, we are told that the Kingdom of Heaven, the Tao, the Path of *Maat,* is to be found within us—which amounts to saying that the election, or selection, of the elite is decided within ourselves, according to how we shrink from or obey our higher impulses.

No sage has ever regarded as particularly fortunate those famous for their knowledge or power, and even less the learned doctors of the law. Unanimously they agree in attributing membership of the elite to those who have rediscovered in the maturity of their adult human consciousness the simplicity of a child.

From what has been said we could define the elite of humanity at present as consisting of those who have at least begun to become aware and critical of the present state of their consciousness, who are not satisfied with their animal humanity and aspire to something higher. The choice is thus already very limited, for even among those who are considered ''cultured,'' how few have any effective notion of the distinction between the human and the suprahuman! Many will not discover the difference until they are already upon the Path, so this we cannot use as a basis for defining the elite; and such classification will be of little interest to those who have in them already the germ of the qualities required. The definition, in fact, is only of value if we have to correct a wrong judgment of the nature of that progress which enables humanity to rise to the suprahuman state.

What matters is not to apply a definition but to observe the characteristic signs of a disposition allotted by destiny or achieved by effort. Among such symptoms are the tendency to sympathize with the sufferings of others, not in the sense of pity, but by opening the heart so that its radiation, without selection or discrimination, acts by itself as a balm of impersonal healing. Other signs are material and spiritual generosity, as opposed to avarice and envy; the feeling or awareness of solidarity; an effective sense of responsibility; and the acceptance of all that makes for simplicity of thought and feeling, looking at all times for the essential point and rejecting perfunctory opinions and fashionable prejudices.

Among the signs we must even include the sense of excess, so long as its motive is not greed for sensual pleasure. For on any higher level it expresses a need to escape our natural and conventional limitations, to pass beyond the precarious human state and touch, even if only for a moment, the suprahuman state.

Since nature cannot tolerate excess, this tendency can only be explained as an instinctive desire to transcend the limits of nature. So if one's motive is not any selfish interest or pleasure, then only guidance is necessary and one will attain the goal, provided one has the heroic courage which is prepared to break the bounds of security in order to reach the infinite.

There can be no question, then, of defining the elite as a chosen body of persons privileged by culture, abilities, or knowledge. It will be composed of those who are searching by every possible means to make contact with ''that which cannot die'' in themselves and in the universe; of those who feel themselves the heirs not of their earthly ancestors, but of those beings who have already reached the stage of ''living incorruptible ones.''

Yet the predisposition to this way is not always conscious in those who have it; often the only evidence of it is an indefinable hunger that no human satisfaction can assuage. But once this tendency is clearly brought to light, the thoughtful man will recognize that it answers the demand of his heart, and by becoming conscious of it he becomes a member of the elite; and this makes him immediately sensitive to the sufferings of others.

For the cause of these sufferings is egocentricity, which makes a man impervious to the vitalizing Fire of the world by wrapping him in that hard shell by which men cut themselves off from one another, like cells in a condition of sclerosis. When such people attempt to acquire wisdom or mastery or powers, their efforts only increase the thickness of their shell and the inflation of their ego. They may form a terestrial elite, but they have no point of contact with the suprahuman realm, where personal ''shells'' are broken and knowledge is the fruit of communion with That Which Is.

The distance between these two paths can be measured by saying that at their beginning there may be no more space between them than the thickness of a razor's edge, but their ends are as far apart as the earth's crust and the sun that warms it.

The Kingdom of ''Heaven,'' that is, of the suprahuman, is liberation from the human by expanding beyond the limits of the personality. The powers thus attained are the miracles wrought by nonresistance and impersonal love. The firmament of the Kingdom, its elite, is constituted by the ''simple'' in heart and thought.

PART FIVE

22

Second Visit to the Cave

The man returned to the cave.

But time has transformed the countryside. The corn had been cut, exposing an arid soil; thickets of thorn had grown up to cover the rocks, and under the yellowing leaves all trace of a path had vanished.

He was disappointed to find no sign of an entrance. Having looked in vain for a landmark, he drew a plan and made some calculations, but without result.

He was about to give up when he noticed hanging on a bush some reddened vine leaves and a few ripe grapes. He approached, but in his greed to get them made a false step, stumbled, and his foot slipped in a hollow. In a moment he was lying at the foot of a staircase, curled up, bruised, and unable to see.

A throaty laugh brought him to his senses.

"Where were you looking for the way in, you careful man? Up in the stars?"

Where did the voice come from? To the visitor's shamefaced glance the room seemed empty. Two bars of light shone in through a couple of slits high up, and threw seductive reflections on the wall. There were shadows too, which gave the impression of living forms and fantastic scenes. Fascinated, the man began watching the wonderful play of light, the combinations of colors and the incessant metamorphoses of the shadows. He forgot both voice and cave.

Then from other slits came inexplicable noises—a strange concert in which voices and sounds of movement were mixed without being confused. Words and familiar tunes could be distinguished, all kinds of animal cries, the sound of wind and stream and thunder, the roar of an avalanche and the faint rustle of wings, and it seemed like an obligation to become absorbed in every one of them.

Then waves of scent came to distract his attention. Searching, he discovered two more slits. An invincible curiosity forced him to recognize the nature of each one of the scents and savors, comparing and analyzing them, quite forgetting both his aim and his journey.

"What are you doing?"

The subterranean voice sounded like a reproach. It broke the spell.

"I was listening—and looking—I was enjoying the fantastic effects of this place. They took me by surprise. Time seems to have passed. I was looking for you, but I could not find you!"

"You cannot find me where I am not. What is it you want?"

"I want your wisdom and advice. But night has come on; how can I reach you?"

"You know the old saying: Explore the inside of the earth. I live in the cave; where are you?"

"I thought I was in the cave."

"You deceive yourself. You do not know the Way of Depth. To find me you must travel downward. Are you quite certain that you are looking for me?"

"Yes, that is what I want with my whole will."

"Your will is just violence, and has no power to find me. The desire which burns in your heart will know what to do. Whatever it commands you to do, obey it. And come—if you dare."

The man came to the center of the cave, where the voice seemed to be, and with all his desire he "let go." The soil gave at the center, and without knowing how, he found himself in the dark cavern at the Master's feet.

The hermit smiled. "So you have managed to escape from the control of the senses?"

The man nodded. "Your voice saved me from that."

"My voice could not have done so if your desire had not already been formulated. It only hastened your choice."

"But is it my choice? At my first visit you threw light on my path, but now all seems confused again."

"If you wish to attain your goal you must, like a navigator, take your bearings and make sure of your direction. I have put three questions to your unconsciousness, and if you can answer them without deceiving yourself, they will serve you for a compass. What are you doing? What do you seek? Where are you?"

"What am I doing? I have been seeking, following the path you showed me."

"But that path was the path of self-knowledge."

"Yes, and it was to give me knowledge of the world. I know my weaknesses now, and my real nature, but unfortunately if I try to control them, I come to a barrier which I cannot cross."

"You think of control as a negation, an act of forcible suppression. Wisdom overcomes the devices of his enemy by taking advantage of its own weaknesses, as animals do in the jungle, or a bush that grows around the curve of a shady rock before reaching for the light."

"That is a childish game, and too distracting when one has the universe to explore!"

"Where did you learn that?"

"Not from myself. I was told by those who say: Forget your body and learn to get out of yourself."

"Good. And what did you do then?"

"I tried to rise above myself. I raised up my mind to the loftiest speculations, and examined every hypothesis in philosophy and science."

"What did you discover?"

"Nothing certain; all was still hypothesis!"

"What did you hope to find?"

"The Laws of the World."

"Do you think they have any connection with intellectual notions?"

"How else could I search?"

"In the only vital consciousness. What became of your meditations?"

"That's a hermit all over! In a busy life one does not have time to meditate."

"Then you had better abandon the quest."

"I cannot; the thirst for knowledge possesses me."

"Then you will be thirsty all your life, for Science cannot give you the key of the universe, nor of Life."

"Where must I seek the answer?"

"In yourself alone."

"I tried that, and failed."

"You neglected the proper method."

"Then I must go back?"

"The journey only becomes quick when one has convinced oneself that all else is vain. If you know yourself in very truth, you will realize that you cannot perform any act or even assimilate any nourishment without expressing the functions of some principle or other. But you find this too simple! Your vanity would prefer to find Wisdom in an ideal world, and your brain professes to invent new ideas. Earthly contingency you regard as a hindrance—which is absurd! You are looking for gold in the clouds, when all the time it is under your feet.

"You must realize that the direct path starts from your daily duties; the tasks for which you have an aptitude are the most suitable ground on which to make your first attempts. It is no use to look far afield for that which you could already have learned by studying the 'appropriate gesture'; but when you have mastered that you will see a wider horizon."

"But even among the most famous craftsmen I have not met any initiates."

"Because they possess a key, but do not know what door it fits. It is not hard to make men adore God in the glory of paradise, but suprahumanity must awaken the sense of sanctity and worship in even the most debased manifestations. That is the fruit of the understanding of matter."

"Then I suppose that the chemist and the surgeon ought to have it?"

"Certainly not; they only dissect. The secret of life is not found with the scalpel, and analysis separates the physical elements from the vital forces which keep them going."

"That I realize; but what prevents me from reaping the fruit of that realization?"

"The complexity of your life. I do not mean your genuine obligations, though even those you can reduce to the inescapable minimum; but you have no clear program, because your goal is not clearly before your eyes.

"There is only one thing necessary, which is to build up your immortal self; and no society or priest or friend can do it for you.

"No one therefore can forbid you to seek this thing which is above every law and takes precedence of every duty. But the means to it is to get rid of obstacles and vitalize your body; then you will feel the sacred Fire beginning to burn brighter."

"It seems to me that you are bringing me back to the vague idealism that you condemned."

"Not at all. I am speaking of your body, for in that alone can you find the nucleus of your Kingdom of Heaven."

"Is success certain?"

"It is certain, for the man who makes it his sole aim. That is why I deplore the complexity of your life."

"But that sole aim is egoism!"

"On the contrary, it is supraegoism; for you cannot bestow the Light until you are yourself luminous."

"But the contingencies of life—"

"Are not obstacles to the man who uses them as exercises in self-mastery. It is a peculiarity of our era that the Quest is not pursued in hermitages. The elect who are called to the higher kingdom must drink the whole cup of human experience, and then rise above it by altruism and not by violence. But this altruism is not an idealistic dream, nor the result of petty charity. It arises naturally from our consciousness of human solidarity, and also from the feeling of power which comes from the certainty of being on the path. For hatred, envy, and stupid selfishness are only reflexes of impotence in a personality which is prey to contradictory aspirations. . . . Have I made the aim clear enough?''

''It is becoming so. So my mistake was in giving in to my ambition for knowledge?''

''Yes, and to the empire of the senses. But that was inevitable, for in attempting to get out of yourself you gave up the endeavor to be master of yourself! He who would play the angel ends by playing the fool.

''But we shall return to that subject later. Consider the second question. What do you seek?''

''I seek that which I am not, and I do that which I would not.''

''You seek the impossible, and yet Divinity is within your reach! Be more exact; what do you seek?''

''I seek the end of my struggles. I seek Peace and Joy and Life.''

''Those are the ends, not the means. Be still more exact; what do you seek?''

''I seek the solution to the problem of existence—the power to rise above the mediocre and the mass, to control my lower powers and attain the higher powers and higher perceptions.''

''At last you are beginning to be frank and state your aim clearly. Your ambition is quite legitimate, for humanity has reached the stage at which the kernel is ripe to open and cast forth its seed. Blessed are those who are part of the kernel, for they shall be the elect, members of the new seed of which all religions have spoken. Every man who feels himself called to this service has a duty to follow it.

''But note this well: to claim membership of the kernel will make you, as the Christ said, ''not of this world''; you will bear the marks of isolation, for the spirit of the kernel is not compatible with that of the mass, and the mass cannot accept its requirements.''

The man listened with some anxiety. ''But the separation will not be violent? It will happen of itself, gradually?''

''Do not deceive yourself. In practice, you can still live in the world; but until you have broken irretrievably with the mentality of the worldly you will never attain your goal.

''There is a direct opposition between the path to the Light and the ways of the World, between the methods of Science and the road of knowledge. They seem to meet sometimes in their results, but their aims are diametrically opposed. The one seeks earthly fruit, the other eternal fruit. Only the latter can justify your ambition.

''And do not suppose that there can be any possible compromise between the two paths. Your struggles and failures are the result of that mistake. There is no bridge either; you must leap, with both feet together, and not look back to the methods of the past. But the crowd will abuse you for it, and accuse you of utopianism and vanity and love of paradox.''

''That I do not mind. Their helplessness shows their methods to be useless; they stand condemned by their failures and by my own. But I am afraid of my own weaknesses; every success I have had was followed by a fall.''

''Before we consider that, let us look at the third question. Where are you?''

''I have no idea! So often I have started off in enthusiasm, and yet I seem to go around in circles and always come back to the same spot.''

The old man gave a mocking laugh. ''Do you think you are the only one? The whole of life goes around in circles and returns upon itself, but never to the same spot. Do you not know the Law of the Spiral in Nature and the Universe? Each time you come to a point which is comparable to some oher, you have comparable difficulties, but with a different rhythm, and with the experience gained before. You have seen the trunk of a tree, and photographs of nebulae?''

''I do not see the connection.''

''Of course not; you neglect the essential and lose yourself in vain speculations without knowledge of Causes. Your curiosity is greedy for intellectual notions. Their superficial aspect impresses you, but it does not awaken in you any awareness of the deeper meaning of their vital correspondences.

''Every fiber, cell, and organ in your body bears the signature of these correspondences. Every function is conscious of itself, but you, who are the sum of them all, know nothing of them!

''Your brain claims to have made a diagram of the physiology of all that lives on earth, by the analysis and resynthesis of notions derived from sense-perception; but Science is continually being obliged to correct the mistakes in these notions, and so your mind gains a wealth of new assertions which are as hypothetical as the old.

''This knowledge is gained by subtraction and only knows Nature by destruction; and at your death it will all go up in smoke.''

''Then does death destroy all understanding?''

''You must distinguish between understanding and knowledge. Knowledge is simply to grasp something; but Understanding is experience engraved in the permanent aspect of what will become your immortal being.''

''But this Understanding cannot exist without formulation in thought!''

''If you had practiced the meditations that I advised, you would have learned that it can exist without any formulation in words. Having evidence of that, you would not need to reason about it. You would know the silent identification of oneself with a law, which animals exemplify when they show awareness that a plant is poisonous, or that an avalanche is coming.

"When this understanding has been acquired, the disciplined mind can transmit it in terms of thought, but only insofar as the listening consciousness can vibrate harmoniously with it; for thought expressed is limited, arrested like the hammer of a piano on a string—which in its turn, however, will vibrate and arouse echos indefinitely."

"But the world I live in is built on thought!"

"That world which you believe in is only a net in which you are caught, and thought is the power that weaves it. It is always setting traps for you in the form of your artificial desires, your imaginary fears, and your useless sufferings. By ingenious arguments it holds your sense of reality prisoner. It makes you resist your Destiny by entangling the guiding thread, and then leaves you helpless and desperate at the confusion."

The man put his head in his hands and began to think. When he raised it there was a gleam of certainty in his eye.

"Master, I have seen through the trick at last! That was what persuaded me to give up your methods as a useless waste of time! What is the best weapon for dealing with it?"

"First of all, a passionate effort to succeed in the meditations I advised you.

"Second, make a holocaust of your intellectual opinions. Give up the relative values of the world of appearances, and in exchange you will find vital consciousness and a sense of absolute values.

"For example, all that happens to you, all that you experience through the senses, you should accept like listening to a simple tune, without thought or intellectual plan, and it should arouse in you a condition which, to begin with, you can call "emotive." It will make you either tranquil or restless, so listen to the tranquillity or the restlessness. That is all. Leave aside analysis and speculation, and simply be.

"Third, in everything look for the central point, the heart, the motive force."

"This program does not fit in with my accustomed rhythm of life; what will give me the strength to accomplish it?"

"The Fire which meditation will arouse."

THE WELL

The man said to the hermit: "What you say seems right, but how will the meaning be made clear? Man is too heavy to climb the heights! His weight always drags him down to earth."

"You are wrong; man is too light. His brain drags him up and makes him float in a cloudy state where all is illusion, unreal by the standards of both spirit and matter."

"Oh, I admit that. Whenever the real vision comes, I am out of my depth and can remember nothing of it."

"Yet look how afraid you are of losing touch with appearances! How it terrifies the animal man to lose his foothold in the void! But to the fully conscious man, what a joy!"

"But you were reproaching me for floating in a cloudy state!"

"Yes, in the cloudy state of idealistic aspirations and intellectual guesswork. I hope, however, to bring you down, so that you will know the heart of things. You must go down inside the earth, inside your own earth; otherwise my teaching can only be superficial."

"You are my Master; show me the way."

The hermit showed him a deep well at the back of the cave.

"First you must do your best to reach the very deepest depth. Go down to the very foundations where sleeps the sacred Fire. If you can arouse it you will know your aim and your power.

"So concentrate the force of your desire, turn in upon yourself, and go down."

"But I can see no foothold!"

Then the man saw the cord, and found it wound several times around his body, and it seemed attached to his navel. He looked up to discover its other end, but it disappeared in the darkness. However, the hermit was holding it firmly to the edge of the well.

"How far must I descend, Master?"

"Until you find your own self in absolute solitude."

"How can I fail to?"

"Remember my words: I said, in absolute solitude. After that, if you can, go to the very bottom. But remain alert, and never for a moment lose consciousness of the cord."

So the man gripped the cord and, overcoming his hesitation, let himself slide down into the well.

After what seemed an endless journey his fall suddenly stopped, but on raising his eyes he found he had descended to only his own height.

"Master, what shall I do?"

No answer, and the weight of his body made it difficult to think. He hoped he would fall lower and so find a foothold. His desire brought him down, bumping painfully against the sides, and he tried to understand the appropriate gesture for his situation. But he listened to his fear, and it brought him up again. He questioned himself, and his thoughts answered. He found he was thinking: "This is not real solitude!"

Again his desire brought him lower; but he was still seeking a foothold, and his thoughts tormented him until he understood their tyranny and deliberately rejected them. For a long time he battled with their insistence; each new image that he repelled returned in another form, imposing like an importunate intriguer, and in the end he tired of the effort.

"How," he cried, "can one uproot that which is part of oneself?"

Then suddenly he saw himself as he was, drawn down by his desire, but held up by the insistence of Ideas, and he realized that this conflict was the source of his difficulty. His amazement was extraordinary, for his thoughts appeared to be outside himself! So that in him which considered his thoughts was independent of them, and did not need them!

He did not formulate this; he experienced it; and that was proof, it was an indescribable certainty which filled him with unexpected peace. He seemed to be warned not to disturb it by any impatience. And as he felt deep within himself for the root of this new "sense," gradually he sank into the Silence.

Perhaps he had a moment of somnolence, for the inner voice awoke him. "Never lose consciousness of the rope!"

Then his feet touched the ground, and he saw himself (whether within or without himself hardly matters). He was in a deep cave like a hollow sphere whose walls moved away as he tried to touch them.

The sky in this sphere was that on which he had at first put his feet, but now it seemed translucent and lit by a diffused light.

The seeker marveled, for a new world was revealed, neither within him nor without, but with no separation between the two.

Then the Fire of the depths awoke; intense heat filled his whole body like a tide of superabundant Life, and Joy flooded him, for all his doubts disappeared, his obstacles melted away, and he perceived the treasure that he had found, which by its power is both end and means, the source of Life, the Living Fire, the One Thing Necessary.

23

Peace

Peace is divine, but men have misused its name. The Earth is one constituent of the universe, but because men see it underneath Heaven, they regard Heaven as its antagonist; for division is the first function of Nature. But just as the two eyes see two images, which are made one in the optic thalamus, so should man forget antagonism and create unity in himself.

Peace is the reconciliation of Heaven and Earth. But to say this to the worldly is a waste of breath, for the worldly man does not know the meaning of either his Heaven or his Earth. His body came from earth, and his Spirit from Heaven desiring to know earth, but the body has denied the Spirit which gives it life. So man looks for God in the starry sky, and makes the intellectual mistake of dividing the Spirit of Heaven from the Spirit of Earth.

He aspires to that which he has already, and is astonished at not finding it; so his hunger remains insatiable, like that of the damned. The fire hidden within him stirs his anger, and that which should have united separates. Thus the antagonism increases, and the only gainers are the personal instincts, which set themselves up in revolt against the sense of reality.

But resistance to the current of Destiny always creates eddies of disturbance, and suffering comes because personal wills prevail against the Will to the Light.

Man says: "War is horrible; let us make peace." But in saying so he surrenders to the most powerful, and the name of Peace is prostituted; for the peace of mere satisfaction and rest is the inertia of a corpse.

True Peace is a continual combat of give and take between the mortal and the eternal, in perfect justice and without violence.

Man has his Heaven within him, and if the human Heaven can attract the divine Heaven, then they mix as water with water and the Kingdom of Heaven is established in man.

The opposition to this union comes from the aggressiveness of the personal instincts, for the separate wants separateness and fears the universal.

As an animal, man is part of the dualism of Nature, and his aggressiveness is the infernal aspect of the Fire incarnate in Nature. Without this Fire there is no combat and no life; the animal instincts express their various characteristics, and each animal species represents one of them, but without being responsible for its aggressiveness since it is bound by the law of Nature's dualism.

Man, at the highest point in Nature, received the gift of consciousness of self; and his brain, having the gift of reason, began to reason about it. He formulated his own law of good and evil according to his own concept of a being subject to the relative and utilitarian conditions of dualism; and thus he created sin, which was relative to his own law.

But consciousness of life submits to the law of life, and both these are cosmic. The law of life is the law of genesis, and at each stage of its evolution this genesis develops a corresponding consciousness, for each stage of development of any organ or creature is the incarnation of a cosmic consciousness.

Man includes all the stages within himself, but the last stage on earth is peculiar to him, for it is the building of his immortal being, the consciousness of his inner Self as a member of the Cosmic Man. This is a function of a higher world; it is the quest for unity.

In a man who has reached this stage everything changes—his aim, his mental attitude, and his law; for man's arbitrary law becomes subordinated to the law of the higher realm in which the only evil is that which prevents unity. The dualistic tendency that most men follow is a hell that he must avoid. His aim and method now is to escape from complementaries, to reach nondivision, nonopposition, and mediation.

The eternal and the mortal are an opposition which seems irreconcilable only to the intellect; for the action of Lucifer which separates them brings in also of necessity the mediator.

But a mediator cannot act from too far outside; if he observes only from a distance, his judgment will not bring peace, and the deeper motives of disagreement will outlast the apparent reconciliation. The true mediator is one who identifies himself with both the opposing tendencies and reconciles them in himself, so that their conflict becomes in him a conscious experience without hatred or violence. Consciousness, the

Permanent Witness of individual experiences, can become the mediator between the eternal and the personal, between heaven and the terrestrial hell.

He who can recognize in himself the instincts which relate him to the lowest, yet without groveling in them, and become aware, but without pride, of that which relates him to the highest, has found the means of concord, for he has conceived the natures of the two antagonists and become their mediator.

Peace is a mystical ferment and its radiance is contagious.

It is a prayer which contains its own answer.

It is an offering on which the Divine descends.

24
Joy

Joy should be sought, for its absence is slow suicide.

Joy is the exultation produced by deliverance from slavery.

But the joys of the world are slavery in themselves, for they are caused by possession of the thing desired, and the fear of loss poisons the joy of possession.

Pleasure is not a joy, only a satisfaction; and not all exaltation is joy; for instance, the exaltation of the brain and senses is only a nervous state, physical plus mental. Sentimental emotion is related to the Personality and therefore not a real joy.

Joy is a movement of the vital Fire, and makes the soul pick up its vibration. But this can only happen if the cause of joy—moral or physical—augments vitality with a gleam of consciousness.

For the soul, being Fire and Light, lives on Fire and Light. Its tendency is to expand to the universal, and therefore its joy is in liberation from personal limitations.

The joys of the world are extinguished by pain, but true Joy is impersonal and therefore knows nothing of pain, in fact uses it as fuel.

Absence of joy is a sign of slackness or satiety or the complacency which neutralizes life. It means absence of sacrifice; and there was wisdom in the popular phrase *feu-de-joie,* ''fire of joy,'' for a bonfire of one's old treasures, letters, and souvenirs.

For the seeker of Light all such loss is a Joy, since it removes an obstacle.

Worldly joy expresses itself externally, but true Joy concentrates itself in order to multiply and increase its heat.

Peace has to be attained, but Joy must be generated.

Sadness is always relative, a negation, a confession of slavery; it is impotant and sterile. Joy is the sign of one who has attained liberation.

Joy is the affirmation of Reality, and such joy is conditioned by nothing but its proper essence, which is the living Fire; when the Fire is active it radiates, and its radiance is Joy.

Joy is the radiance of a Sun. It may seem dark or bright according to the object which reflects it, but Creation gazes upon it and is illumined. In the silence of Heaven it expands and is added to the wealth of the world.

This joy is the wealth of the sages, and the consciousness of the Cosmic Man.

25

"Son of Man" and "Son of God"

Life is a cyclic movement of continual regeneration. Each of its appearances is an individuation of cosmic functions, and each individual incarnates the faculties of assimilation and reproduction.

Physical appearances are a reflection of the activity of life on the plane of principles, and to understand this reflection is to know the working of Causes.

It is madness to try to exploit the vital powers for personal ends. The world admires those who are so mad, but death is the end of them.

The sage espouses harmony, and accepts hindrances as a means of working for liberation. The world scouts the sage, but for him death is the entrance into indestructible life.

So the question remains: What is Life?

Life is the Divine Presence, the Word made flesh, Whose becoming is genesis.

The flesh, thus living, receives an irresistible current of life from the conjunction of Cosmic powers, and creates in matter a reflection of their functions.

These functions seem like a natural process predestined and irreversible, but which can be temporarily halted in forms.

Form is destructible, but Life is not; it knows nothing of death. It destroys the mortal mercilessly, and decomposes the destructible. But the indestructible remains.

Being immortal, it carries within it the means of regeneration even as the means of destruction.

There is only one stream, but each thing draws from the stream a different water, according to the quality of its vessel, that is, its desire.

Each new activity of life proceeds from a formal death. The grain that does not rot in the ground cannot grow; but its product can only be other grain like the first.

Life is consciousness, and enlarges itself by extending the limits of form.

Man has the power to generate in his lifetime his immortal being, and thus when his successive limiting forms have been destroyed and his inharmonious elements consumed, he will rise from his ashes.

Matter, which belongs within the limitations of form, does not desire this regeneration. This gestation of the immortal being requires an impulse from outside Nature, and the Life which produces this regeneration is above Nature.

This is the mystery of the expression "Son of Man."

The life transmitted by woman is earthly life; the fruit of every womb is mortal.

The paternal seed fixes the mortal nature, yet it is in itself an individual manifestation of the Light, by which the creating Spirit acts through the father to create an individual.

Thus the "Son of Man," though he must die like the "son of woman," has within him the immortal seed of resurrection and immortality.

For the world this will remain an enigma, and may be thought harsh and pointless; but He who called himself "the Son of Man" did not hesitate to confront his followers with this riddle.

Also he called himself "Son of Man" and later "Son of God," but he never called the "son of woman" a "Son of God."

For Nature is feminine and passive; it receives stimulation from the creating Spirit. But the Spirit is male and active, since it creates and give life.

The "sons of woman," that is, of Nature, are vowed to the life of appearances, and "the greatest of these" is only the "forerunner" of him who has within him the seed of Christhood. But the latter is "the Son of Man," who by sacrifice is to lose his mortal nature and raise up in human nature the consciousness of the Divine.

At each stage of life the animal man makes a step to recover his immortal name, and the last stage is that of "Son of God," meaning "born of God"; for, according to the scriptures,* those who have received the word of God are called gods; and He who has received the divine Logos and become an incarnation of it is indeed a "son of God."

The expression "Only Son" refers to the very high mystery of the "Unique Sacrifice," to the mission of Him who was sent by the

*John 10:34-36.

"Father" as an incarnation of the Cosmic Man and as Mediator until the end of time on earth.

Thus onto the natural life of earth is grafted the spiritual life of the higher world, the Kingdom of Heaven, and this is the crown, on earth, of the human-animal kingdom, which developed out of the three other kingdoms, the mineral, vegetable, and animal.

The scepter is offered to every man who, by sacrificing his personal limitations, can learn to draw from the river of life the essentials of rebirth.

26

Signature

Explanation is one thing, meditation another; both are necessary. So we shall let the heart speak, without concern for what men may say.

The Spirit "bloweth where it listeth," and not where men desire.

Truth is that which is, not what men imagine.

The Destiny of the Earth is written in the Sun and Moon, and not in the science of men.

The heredity of the "person" is written in his liver, not in human records.

His destiny can be read in his eyes, his hands, his face, but these are to men a secret cipher.

His true "name" is the impulse which brought him to earth; only his appearance has a name among men.

The place which has drawn him down to human earth is his country of adoption.

If the throne of his heart is empty, then the end of life for him will have all the horror of endless exile.

But if his heart is the throne of his immortal Self, then his true country is the place in Heaven whence he descended, and his place of exile is among men.

Appendix I
The Functional Relationship
of Bodily Organs

VITAL STATES OF THE ORGANS

To understand an organ one must consider not only its constitution and function, but also the conditions required for proper fulfillment of the function. These are:

1. The mutual relationship of the organ and the blood
2. Its relation, in terms of energy, with the sources of vital force and with the other organs
3. The functional groups to which it belongs
4. The neighboring region, and the organs affected by proximity.

We have put first its relation with the flow of blood and with the currents of energy because it is these two forces which give life to the organism. On their quality and balance depends the health or sickness of the whole body.

Blood and energy are two vitalizing powers, each with its own circuits and conduits. Their circulation is like that of a tree, which has its roots in earth and spreads out toward heaven, the circuit of the sap rising up the trunk from root to leaves and returning to the root again. We can thus speak of the Vital Tree of Energy and the Vital Tree of the Blood.

The Vital Tree of Energy consists of the spinal marrow, which has its roots in the region of the sacrum and spreads out in the brain, beginning from the medulla oblongata. The system of sensitive and motor nerves branches out on either side of the spine, and is complemented by the two circuits of the Sympathetic and Parasympathetic, which are the agents of dilation and contraction.

The more subtle circuit of energy, as revealed by the sensitive points along the "meridians" of the system of acupuncture, shows how each organ depends upon another for the energy which regulates the performance of its functions.

The Vital Tree of the Blood is the tree of respiration and exchange between interior and exterior.

The Chinese say: "The roots are in the kidneys, and the tendrils in the lungs."

The lower calls to the higher, and attracts what the higher takes.

The higher takes air and fire from outside and breathes them out again.

The lower expels the superfluous water.

The heart receives on the right the impure blood, and sends it to be revitalized in the lungs; on the left it receives the revitalized blood and distributes it to the body.

The upper circuit is: heart—head—heart.

The lower circuit is: heart—body—kidneys—body—heart.

In passing through the liver, the constituents of the blood are transformed according to the requirements of the twelve specific types of energy.

The kidneys keep the water filtered and in due proportion.

The blood is here considered as the vehicle which receives the breath and transforms the air and fire breathed in by the lungs, specializing them to the particular nature of the individual. The organs which are part of this "tree of exchange" work together in the transformation, and regulate the distribution of water so as to keep a proper balance of fluidity.

As vehicle of the animal soul, and distributor of animal life throughout the organism, the blood works through the main circuits of the vascular system; the veins, arteries, and capillaries.

This activity of the blood, as receiver of the breath and animator of the body, is discharged by the functions included under the name of "respiration." Its mechanical aspect as inspiration and expiration belongs to the vegetative functions of the "tree of exchange"; but the assimilation of what is breathed in, and the transformation of the blood which results, are part of the seven genetic functions which regulate the organism.

The purity and vitality of the whole body depend on that of the blood, but conversely, all the organs cooperate toward its continual regeneration.

Its flow is regulated by the heart, but the seat of regeneration of its corpuscles is the spleen, which has a luni-solar action upon the red and white corpuscles and a Saturnian function in transformation.

It is individualized and adapted to personal characteristics in the liver.

Its "mother" or source of energy is the "Master of the Heart."

Its "nurse," which brings it the lunar chyle, is the small intestine.

It is purified by the lungs, which aerate and vitalize it; the liver, which destroys toxins and eliminates foreign matter; and the kidneys, which filter and distribute water.

It is transmuted and set free as energy in the marrow and certain glands.

COORDINATION OF FUNCTIONS

The object of this extremely brief study is to give a synthetic view of the coordination of the organic functions, and show how all the elements in our body depend on one another.

Our physical life is maintained, regenerated, and reproduced by the balanced working of seven functions related to metabolism, which we shall here call genetic functions. Each function is discharged by a group of four organs. It is important to know these groups, for the four organs which discharge the same function, each according to its capacity, are brought into relationship by the function.

These are the seven functions, with the seven groups of four organs which discharge them:

1. DIGESTION:
>
> Mouth
> Stomach
> Small Intestine
> Large Intestine

2. SELECTION (purification by separation):
>
> Small Intestine
> Large Intestine
> Liver
> Kidneys

3. EXCRETION:
>
> Large Intestine
> Bladder
> Lungs
> Skin

4. INDIVIDUALIZATION (assimilation):
>
> Small Intestine
> Liver
> Lungs
> Kidneys (including the generative glands and region)

5. TRANSFORMATION OF THE BLOOD:
>
> Liver
> Spleen
> Lungs
> Marrow

6. GENERATION OF SUBSTANCE:
    Small Intestine (chyle)
    Kidneys (in relation with genital region)*
    Spleen (blood corpuscles)
    Genitals (sperm and ova)
7. TRANSMUTATION OF BLOOD INTO ENERGY:
    Marrow and certain glands

When a function is carried out by several organs, all are affected to some extent by the proper or improper manner of its discharge. For example, the tongue reflects the condition of all the digestive organs; the skin reflects the condition of all the excretory organs; and the insufficiency or excess of intestinal excretion is influenced by the three other excretors, and vice versa. (In China a definite relationship is considered to exist between the lungs and the large intestine.) Thus a single function in its different phases has repercussions on all the organs which work together to discharge it.

THE REGIONS OR AREAS

Each organ is surrounded by an area in which it continually generates and regenerates itself. (Medicine is now beginning to take notice of this, in connection with intersticial tissue.) This area constitutes its atmosphere, just as the sphere of a star extends well beyond its globe to the extreme limit of its radiations. These radiations constitute its sphere of vital exchange, and it can thus be penetrated by the radiations of other stars. Our solar system, in fact, is composed of spheres of emanation and radiation rotating within the immense radiant sphere of their sun.

Thus the Moon, as it revolves around the Earth, forms part of the radiant sphere of the Earth, which itself extends beyond the sphere of influence formed by the Moon's orbit.

This is how planetary influences should be thought of, and how the interdependence of organs should be thought of, allowing for the importance of the areas surrounding them. It also explains why, if the spleen is removed, that area can fulfill the function of the organ and sometimes even create other little spleens.

This extension of organic influences explains the affinities which exist between several organs belonging to the same area; and it also explains the network of meridians of energy which expresses in the skin the sensibility of the various organs. For the skin is the outermost apparent "sphere" of the body, and everything radiates outward to the skin, not only the sweat

---

*According to an old Chinese tradition there is a functional relationship between the kidneys and the formation of the bone marrow. See G. Soulié de Morand, *Acupuncture chinoise* (Paris: Mercure de France, 1939).

but the various exhalations, whether solid (skin, crusts), liquid (perspiration), subtle (odors and tactile sensibility), feverish, energic, magnetic, etc.

This function of exteriorization is complemented by a function of interiorization, an inspiration and absorption, which makes the role of the skin like that of the earth's crust or the leaves of a tree, where a continual interchange takes place between the creature and its atmosphere, between the organ and its area, thus making possible the metabolism necessary to life.

The respiration of the skin is so important that a man cannot live if two-thirds of his skin is destroyed. But each organ has its own envelope or skin, which plays a similar part: for the lungs the pleura, for the intestines the peritoneum, for the brain the meninges.

This envelope, with the radiations it emits, forms part of the area of an organ, and so do the glands which manufacture the liquids needed for its functioning. The nature of the function is revealed by the taste and other properties of these liquids; those of the mouth and intestine are alkaline, those of the stomach for the most part acid, those of the pancreas sweet, those of the gallbladder bitter, the tears salt, and so forth. Each of these liquids is secreted in response to the "appetite," or emotion, or an organic or psychic center.

Thus each area is, like the areas of the sky, the scene of a continual interplay of influences, of attractions and repulsions and their mutual repercussions.

The organs influenced by any one area are in mutual affinity and dependence.

The four areas of the organism are (1) on the left side, the stomach, spleen, pancreas, and heart; (2) on the right side, the liver, gallbladder, and pancreas; (3) in the upper part of the trunk, the lungs and bronchi, the tracheal artery, the larynx, and the heart with the vessels of the respiratory circuit; (4) in the lower part of the abdomen, the small and large intestine, with the peritoneum, and the kidneys in their mechanical aspect.

At the two poles there are the two complementary glands, the thyroid and adrenals, and the two polar worlds, the brain and sex.

At the northern pole, the thyroid is in relation with the extreme North, which is the pituitary, and with the brain.

At the southern pole, the adrenals are in relation with the sexual glands and functions. The functions of these "polar" glands are, conversely, related to the glands and functions of the opposite pole.

The two double organs in the body, the lungs and kidneys, have a double role, both mechanical and energic. This can be confirmed from the table (page 197) showing the relations of the vital trees of energy and of the blood.

Finally, the organs which appear to be mere vessels or containers, such as the bladder and gallbladder, have important functions in stimulating the organs on which they depend, the kidneys in the case of the bladder, and the liver in that of the gallbladder.

There are no completely passive containers in the body. Each organ by the mere fact of its existence has two aspects, one masculine or active, the other feminine or passive; for not only does every quality find its complement somewhere in Nature, but each carries its complementary aspect in itself. The organs are no exception to this rule.

THE FOUR SONS OF HORUS

We must now consider an important aspect of our bodily organs, which is revealed to us by the Egyptian sages.

The Egyptians, before embalming a mummy, used to remove the four viscera, which are the incarnation of the animal *Ka*s, of the principal organic functions. These they put into four vases, later called ''canopic,'' the four lids having three animal heads and one human head.

The human-headed vase was called Imset, and contained the liver. The baboon-headed vase was called Hapi, and contained the lungs. The jackal-headed vase was called Duamutef, and contained the stomach, and occasionally also the large intestine. The hawk-headed vase was called Qebhsenuf, and contained the small intestine.

These organs were called the Sons of Horus because their functions, when man becomes aware of them, contribute to the realization of the Horus in man, that is, of man's complete and immortal consciousness.

They are therefore represented at the judgment of the deceased as elevated on a lotus; that is to say, sublimated or subtilized, having lost all their perishable elements and become pure consciousness.

Each belongs to one of the four regions of the body, for which its function is characteristic.

The canopic vases did not contain either the polar organs (brain and sex) or the kidneys, which in their energic aspect belong to the sexual system.

Duamutef (Jackal, Stomach)

The real meaning of this name is shown by the way it is written on the sarcophagus of Amenophis II, *d•wa•mut•f*, in which the hieroglyph *wa* represents a knot coming untied. *Mut* (meaning both Mother and Vulture) symbolizes the function of decomposition which takes place in the stomach as in a womb and makes possible the generation of a new life. This is also the function of the jackal, which converts putrefying matter into vital nourishment.

This is the first stage of any genesis, and the ''Opener of the Ways'' (the god Wep-wawet) is Anubis the jackal.

The same inscription says that Duamutef "gives the king his heart." Now, the Egyptian name of the stomach is *ra-ib*, which means "gate of the heart." This mysterious title is explained by the important relation between the heart and the group stomach-spleen-pancreas, which is confirmed by Chinese medical lore.

Imset (Man, Liver)

The name Imset is related to the production by the liver of *set*, the separating fire of the god Set, the bile. The word for liver is *miset* or *merset*, usually written with the sign *mr*, which represents a canal or reservoir; and of course the liver is the reservoir of the "water of Set," the bile, which it canalizes into the gallbladder. Thence the bile runs into the small intestine, where it makes possible the separation of subtle and coarse, of pure and impure.

The symbol of the human head shows the two aspects of the liver; in its psychic role it is the seat of the Personality, whose innate and inherited characteristics are engraved in it. Second, this indicates the mutual reaction of brain and liver whenever the Personality receives a shock.

The Egyptians also said that "Imset leads his brethren," and that he "makes green" (*rwd*, meaning to grow, to vegetate). By its separative action the bile creates the chyle, which is the basic nourishment of vegetative life.

Imset "leads his brethren," who are the other animal functions, because he is the seat of the personal impulses which can direct or thwart the animal instincts. Further, he is in constant touch with the cerebral will, which is continually colored by the individual character.

The liver is the seat of the subconscious personality, the Automaton, but also of the Permanent Witness.

Hapi (Baboon, Lungs)

This name means "circuit" or "Solstice." It refers to the arterial circuit heart-lungs-heart, by which the blood recovers its vitalizing power. It is also the function which maintains a continual exchange, by inspiration and expiration, between the life of man and the life of the surrounding world. The baboon, which is so responsive to the influence of sun and moon, is a symbol of this circuit. But it also symbolizes the animal side of man, his animal life, with the unconscious impulses of the Automatic Self, whose seat is in fact in the lungs. This is the Chinese *pro*, which is located in the lungs.*

---

*See Appendix II.

Qebhsenuf (Hawk, Small Intestine)

This name means literally "He refreshes his brethren," and this organ produces the white lunar chyle, which refreshes the blood and purifies the bitter fires, whether consuming or separating, of the other organs. It provides nourishment which has been "individualized," that is, made directly assimilable by the organism.

The white hawk of Horus, which is the symbol of the chyle, signifies its volatile quality, in the sense of subtlety and rising up continually toward the heart, from whence it is distributed through the body by the lymph, which it also nourishes.

Qb means "folds"; *qbh* means "refreshment." "*Qebhit*" is the uraeus on the royal crown, whose head stands up out of many folds. The other name for the uraeus is *ar•t,* that which rises up.

Qebhut is the daughter of Anubis (the jackal of the stomach), and of course the chyle is the daughter of the chyme produced by the stomach. This chyle "feeds the flesh and bones," as the Egyptians say, whereas the function of Duamutef, both as jackal and vulture, was to devour them.

RELATIONSHIPS OF BODILY ORGANS

	Vital Tree of Energy	Vital Tree of Blood	Influence of Proximity	Functional Groups
STOMACH (Duamutef, jackal)*	spleen pancreas gall bladder		spleen pancreas heart	**Digestion:** mouth, small & large intestines
LIVER (Imset, man) acts on acts on sex	gall bladder spleen	spleen	gall bladder pancreas	**Selection:** small & large intestines, kidneys **Assimilation:** small intestine, lungs, kidneys, sex **Transmutation of blood:** spleen, lungs, spinal marrow
SPLEEN	liver stomach pancreas	liver	stomach pancreas **heart**	**Transmutation of blood:** liver, lungs, marrow **Generation of substance:** small intestine, kidneys, sex
SMALL INTESTINE (Qebhsenuf, hawk)*	heart large intestine		large intestine periteneum kidneys	**Digestion:** mouth, stomach, large intestine **Selection:** liver, kidneys, large intestine **Assimilation:** liver, lungs, kidneys, sex **Generation of substance:** kidneys, spleen, sex
LARGE INTESTINE	lungs		small intestine peritoneum kidneys	**Digestion:** mouth, stomach, small intestine **Selection:** small intestine, liver kidneys **Excretion:** bladder, lungs, skin
LUNGS (Hapi, baboon)*	large intestine heart	kidneys	bronchi tracheal artery larynx	**Excretion:** large intestine, bladder, skin **Assimilation:** small intestine, liver, kidneys & sex **Transmutation of blood:** liver, spleen spinal marrow
KIDNEYS	bladder Master of the heart sex	lungs	small & large intestines bladder adrenals heart	**Selection:** small & large intestine, liver **Assimilation:** small intestine, liver, lungs, sex **Generation of substance:** small intestine, spleen, sex
BLADDER	kidneys	opposite the mouth	kidneys sexual region	**Excretion:** large intestine, lungs, skin
HEART	small intestine lungs	lungs kidneys liver spleen	spleen stomach lungs arteries Master of the heart & Spiritual Heart	

*Acts on heart.

Appendix II
Psychospiritual States in Different Traditions*

When considering the relationship of psychic and spiritual states to organic functions, it is important to bear in mind also the general conditions on levels more subtle than the physical.

The breath of life (in Egyptian, the universal *Ba*) is breathed in by the lungs and individualized by the blood into an animal vital force (in Egyptian, the animal *Ba*); this is the inferior or "sensitive" soul, the Hebrew *nefesh*. It corresponds to the Chinese *pro* which is the unconscious vital energy of the cells, the organs, and the sex,** and resides in the lungs.

The astral or "etheric" body, corresponding to the popular notion of a ghost (*linga-sharira* among the Hindus, and in Egyptian the Shadow, *Khaibit*), has its seat in the spleen. It is related to the Akasha, the world or state which holds the records of all the pictures or imaginings in our universe, and this justifies the idea of the spleen as seat of the imagination.

The individual vital force, which engraves in the liver the characteristics of the personality and the paternal heredity, is the intermediate or "personal" *Ka* of the Egyptians. The Chinese call it "roun" and situate it in the liver, and define its manifestations as "personal vital energy, personal vital needs and tendencies, conscious sexual needs." In actual fact this consciousness belongs to the Automatic Self, the mortal ego, and in relation to the Ego-Consciousness it is a form of subconsciousness, so long as the latter, which also reacts in the liver, is not awakened.

---

*See chapter 4, Soul and Consciousness. For the Psychospiritual States in Different Traditions, see also Isha Schwaller de Lubicz, *Her-Bak: Egyptian Initiate*. New York: 1978, Inner Traditions.

**G. Soulié de Morand, *Acupuncture chinoise* (Paris: Mercure de France, 1939).

The mental state (Sanskrit *manas*) has two aspects. The brain is the organ of the one, and in its different localizations is connected with all the operations of the lower mind. The other belongs to man's immortal consciousness and his spiritual intelligence, and has no physical organ, but uses relay stations suitable to its different modes of expression.

The intuitive state (which in Hinduism begins with *buddhi*) has its physical relay stations in the pineal gland and in the region of the heart; it is related to the Chinese *chen*, translated as "consciousness" or "the spiritual spark which relates man to the universe." This state is located by the Chinese and Egyptians in the heart.

The words "soul" and "spirit," as used in Christian countries, are so vague that we must now request the reader to permit the adoption of two terms from ancient Egypt, *Ba* and *Ka*—first, because the metaphysical meaning of these words is strictly defined, and second because the philosophical notions connected with them will make it possible to explain their different aspects better than in any other way. The following description is quoted from the Commentaries on *Her-Bak*.*

There is good reason to emphasize the Egyptian form of this teaching, because the ancient texts, hieroglyphs, and pictures remaining unaltered are the witnesses of an immutable tradition.

THE SOUL IN ANCIENT EGYPT

The different constituents of human nature are given different names in each religious tradition, and their number and classification may even vary between the schools of a single tradition, but this in no way impugns the reality of our knowledge of them.

The occult elements of human nature are stages or modes of consciousness which do in fact exist, however they may be named or classified; and in the knowledge and experience of these several states consist the various degrees of Mastership, regardless of any differences of terminology. To study them in theory, however, does require a knowledge of the terms to be employed.

The word "soul" is too vaguely inclusive, and will lead to illusions when the discrimination between different states of consciousness is not possible owing to ignorance. At the other extreme, a too subtle analysis is intellectually irritating, and that too is an obstruction in the way of self-knowledge.

The principal metaphysical states of man are mentioned by the Egyptians, but are not analyzed so intricately as by the Hindus. Such analysis was unnecessary because the hieroglyphic symbols can express the different aspects of a single principle according to how they are used, in

*Isha Schwaller de Lubicz, *Her-Bak: Egyptian Initiate*. New York: 1978. Inner Traditions.

groups or severally, and in such a method there is less risk of error than in studying separately constituents which cannot properly be isolated.

The intricacy, however, is no less great when we consider the different occult meanings of our spiritual constituents. It is not hard for the imagination to comprehend the two extreme conditions of the human composite, the most spiritual on the one hand, and on the other the nearest to the body, the Shade or Ghost, the "emotional body," which preserves our likeness and bears the traces of our psychic life.

But it is more difficult to define the intermediate factors, which have something both of the higher and of the lower natures, such as the different aspects of the *Ba* and *Ka,* which are somtimes spoken of separately and sometimes taken together under a single name.

The definitions of these two must always be relative to each other, since they can only refer to one aspect in its relations to the other.

Ba, in relation to *Ka,* is the animating spirit.

Ka, in relation to *Ba,* is the individualization of consciousness in the more or less gross or subtle states of being, and makes it possible to stabilize the animating spirit.

Ba gives the breath of life; its characteristic is nonfixity, and it always needs a support.

Ka is a principle of fixity, of fixation and attraction; it is the power which can attract, stabilize, and transform the vital or animating principle, *Ba.*

The word *bka,* meaning the impregnation or fecundation of a female, shows how these two factors must be brought together for there to be a conception, which is an incarnation of the essential and specific *Ka,* given by the seed, and animated by the vital breath of the *b-.*

"It must not be forgotten that all comes from the One, and all factors or states of being are only manifestations of the One, despite the different names which are given them to express Its different aspects. These aspects can themselves appear interchangeable, according to their mutual modes of action and reaction in all the triads of "manifestation" which have issued from the original trinity. Hence there may be interchange of names between different functions.

Thus with *Ba* and *Ka* there is continual interchange, each playing now the active part, and now the passive.

Being thus warned against interpreting them schematically, we can study the respective characters of *Ba* and *Ka.*

Ba is the impersonal aspect of the soul because it is the universal aspect, but it is conditioned by its affinities with the *Ka,* and these are determined by the circumstances of birth.

In the account of our becoming, *Ba* and *Ka* are the second and third states or principles, manifesting the Trinity, which is first creative, then formative, then regenerative. The first principle is not *akh*, as the usual terminology would lead one to suppose, but *a*, which contains virtually the two aspects (activity, passivity, *àa* or *ia*) of the Original Source, the Creative Word. *Akh* is the original Power begotten in the darkness of matter and overcoming it in its quality of "Light emerging from darkness."

The second factor, *Ba*, was considered in Egypt under three aspects, as the Universal Soul, the Natural Soul, and the Human Soul, but it has in itself a dual character.

For just as in the original Trinity TWO has a dual character, in that it shares in the divine essence of the ONE from which it proceeds, but also has a particular or individual aspect because of its part in Nature, which it is going to "cause" by its duality; so too *Ba* is both universal, and at the same time particularized in the human being. Yet, since its nature is spiritual, it remains indivisible; that is to say, if it ceases to be individualized, it returns to union with its source.

Ba, like *Ka*, has three aspects:

1. *Ba* is the cosmic soul, the Spirit of Fire, which gives life to the world in all its parts. Originally there is *Ba*, and at the end there is *Ba*, and between the beginning and end *Ba* is in everything, being the breath which creates life. Hence the spirit of *Ba* is in all the constituents of the world and in its final perfection.

2. *Ba* is the Natural Soul stabilized in the bodily form, and its character is Osirian; that is, it is subject to cyclic renewal. This aspect is symbolized by the ram with horizontal horns.

3. *Ba* is also represented by a bird with a human head, and this is the symbol of the human soul, which comes and goes between heaven and earth, wandering near its body until the purification of its *Ka-djet*, or glorious indestructible body, which it can then take on.

The three aspects of *Ka* may be understood as follows:

Originally, *Ka* is the Formal Element which gives form to Substance and thus creates Matter. It is the spiritual principle of fixity, which will become the basis of all manifestation, and through the ages of Becoming will undergo innumerable modifications from the basest of forms to the perfection of the indestructible body.

Ka as a cosmic power is in essence the idea of the hieroglyph of the Bull. As bearer of the generative power it provides the inherited individual quality, whether in the original creative source or in terrestrial procreators. *Ka* therefore is the bearer of all the powers of manifestation, the motive force of the universal functions. The Egyptians also called it the "Father of the fathers of the Neters (principles)," for *Ka* is the principle which realizes (makes real) continuous creation; without it the Father would have no effective power, and by it the Son reveals the face of his Father. By it all things receive their ''names.''

The *Ka*s of the Sun, Ra, are its active properties; the *Ka*s of any kind of food are its vitalizing qualities. For the *Ka* is the source of all appetites.

''All the aspects of *Ka* are to be found in man, but not all are under his control. The higher qualities of the *Ka*, which feed upon the subtle fires of the marrow, only become incorporated in him when he has knowledge of and mastery over them.

The animal *Ka*s reside in the intestines, and the appetites of which they are the incarnation remain for a certain time after death. It was for these *Ka*s that funeral food was offered. But the higher *Ka* of a man is superior to these animal *Ka*s.

We can now see the three aspects of the *Ka:*

First, the original *Ka*, creator of all the others; then the *Ka*s of Nature, mineral, vegetable, and animal; then the individualized *Ka* of man, which includes his inherited character and his own signature, and so determines his destiny.

In the human realm the *Ka* was also regarded by the Egyptians under three aspects: on the universal level, as the origin of man; in the King, as microcosm, type and symbol of the perfected man; and in the ordinary man, not yet perfected.

We can now speak of the human *Ba* as of an individual soul, which, thanks to its *Ka*, becomes an Entity.

Ba, a pure and formless spirit, must always have a support in order to manifest, and this support is the selective affinity of the thing it has to animate; and the affinity is determined and characterized by the *Ka*.

It is the characteristics of the *Ka* which make the choice of circumstances for incarnation, as also of nourishment and surrounding atmosphere; for its affinity is only with things of its own specific nature, and this applies also after the death of the body, both as regards the vital elements of the tomb offerings and the surroundings.

The *Ka*, which is the stable element in a man, is distinguished from the *Ka*s of other men by the specific qualities of its own selective affinity. The universal *Ba* is in constant contact with the man whom it animates, and with his *Ka;* but the *Ka*, by assimilating it, generates a new being, which is the individualized soul, which remains divine, incorruptible, and therefore immortal, and yet is governed by the affinity which it now has for the characteristics of its *Ka*. This is what we call the higher *Ka*.

The individualized *Ba* is thus the most spiritual element in man, for by its divine nature it is his link with the Creator. For this reason it will always be incomprehensible to the thinking faculty, whose relative nature cannot make contact with the Spirit. Thus too it is impossible to pin down and define this *Ba*-soul, or enclose it in a body; for it is incommensurable and indivisible, free, unfixed, and unaffected by the vicissitudes of the human being whose only link with it is a link of consciousness.

It is hard to distinguish the different aspects of the *Ka*, because their difference lies not in their source or cause, but only in their effects. If the light of the sun is reflected by several mirrors made of different metals, it will take on different colors and qualities from the different mirrors. Thus, though every *Ka*-entity issues forth from the one source of *Maat* [consciousness-truth], each is characterized in the man to whom it is incarnated, by the signatures of the vital forces (the natural, organic, and instinctive *Ka*s) which it finds in him, and by the innate consciousness of his being.

Thus the *Ka* is his agent of consciousness, the Permanent Witness of the transformations of his being; it is the personality engraved in the liver and signed upon the skin by Seshat; it shares the emotional reactions which are felt by the heart and by the *Ka*s of the animal body; it is fed by the *Ka*s of foodstuffs, and enriched by the double *nefer,* the double current of ''fire'' in the vertebral column.

A man ignorant of his own spiritual world has little or no contact with his divine *Ka*. His personal *Ka* is brought down to the whole of his lower *Ka*s; therefore he will become, after death, his own shade or ghost. But the quest for the spiritual springs of action, and the enlargement of consciousness, can modify the character of his ''personal'' *Ka* until the spiritual faculties are awakened and it makes contact with its divine *Ka;* and this proportionately diminishes the tyranny of the inferior *Ka.*

This account of the aspects of *Ba* and *Ka* is closer to reality than all the theoretical explanations that would have had to be given to render intelligible the various aspects of what is commonly called ''the soul.'' It would be wise to think about them frequently and deeply until their reality becomes apparent.

In this work the word ''soul'' has been used for the highest spiritual aspect of the *Ba.* The individualized soul, or Spiritual Witness, which may also be called the Witness of the Impersonal Self, has been called the ''divine *Ka*.'' The Permanent Witness, or Personal Consciousness, corresponds to the Intermediate *Ka.*

The inferior *Ka* comprises the ''psychological consciousness'' of the Automaton (physical, emotional, and mental). The animal *Ka*s correspond to the organic consciousness, including the essential functional consciousness, which the Egyptians called ''the four sons of Horus.''

Index

Abyss, 130
Accomplishments
    approprite gesture, 118-119
    concentration, 114-116
    generosity, 124-126
    sense of Presence, 113-114
    serenity, 116-118
    silence, 119-122
    thankfulness, 122-124
Action, Master of, 153
Acupuncture, meridians of, 26
Adrenal glands, 21
Akasha, mirror of, 45
Alternation, and pendulum, 95-99
Altruism, 133-134
Animal heat and energy, sources, 26-27
Appropriate gesture, 118-119
Assimilation, 191
Astral body, 199
Astrology, 18
Atrabile, 22
Automatic Self, 18, 39
Automaton, 17, 33-37, 40
    and conduct, 105, 108
    constitution of, 19-22
    and duel, 43-49
    and knowledge, 66-67
    and mediation, 102-103
    and pendulum, 98
    and Way of the Heart, 56, 57

Ba, 199, 201-204
Baboon, 195
Back, 21

Becoming, 34
Being, bodies of, 19-20
Bile, 22, 57, 103-104
Blood, 22
    transformation, 191
    transmutation into energy, 192
    Vital Tree of, 189-190
Bodily organs
    coordination of functions, 191-192
    regions or areas, 192-194
    sons of Horus, 194-196
    vital states, 189-191
Body
    conscious reanimation, 39-41
    orientation, 21-22
    of physical being, 19-20
Brain, 103-104
    and sex, 92
Breath of life, 199

Cave, visits to, 85-90, 167-175
Chuang-tse, 129, 131
Chyle, 20, 26
Circuits, control of, 25-26
Compassion, 132-133
Concentration, 114-115, 129
Concern, personal, 128-130
Condemnation, 12
Conduct, 105-109
Consciousness, 2
    in man, 32-37
    origins, 31
    in universe, 31-32
Conscious Self, 46, 57

Contraction, and dilation, 97-98
Creative Word, 2, 3

Depth, 40
Desire, vs. love and need, 91-94
Digestion, 191
Digestive organs, 20
Dilation, and contraction, 97-98
Discernment, 75-76
Divine Compassion, 132, 135
Divine *Ka. See* Permanent Witness
Divine Presence, 59
Divine Wisdom, 3-4
Double power (*sekhemti*), 50
Duamutef, 194-195
Duel, 43-47, 55
     and conduct, 106
     stages of, 47-49

Elite, 161-164
     vs. mass of humanity, 11
Emerald Table, 40, 64
Emotion, and sentimentality, 138-139
Energy
     and animal heat, sources, 26-27
     transmutation of blood into, 192
     Vital Tree of, 189
Etheric body, 199
Excretion, 191
Eyes, 22

Face, 22
Fault, 12
Fire, 156
     and joy, 181
     of life, 27-28
First cause, 2
Fountain, and gifts of Spirit, 63-64
Freedom, of individual search, 11-12
Function, and knowledge, 65

Gallbladder, 103
Generation, of substance, 192
Generosity, 124-126
Gesture, appropriate, 118-119
Gold, 50
Gratitude, 124
Great question, 13-15

Hallucinations, 120
Hapi, 195

Hate, 80-81
Head, 21-22
Heart, 20, 24-25, 27, 57
     mediation of, 59-61
     and serenity, 116
Heart-kidneys-sex circuit, 25
Heart-lungs-heart circuit, 25
Heaters, 25
Height, 40
Hermes, Emerald Tablet, 40, 64
Hippocrates, 79
Horus, 22, 27
     sons of, 194-196
Humors, 22-23, 83
Ida, 26, 27
Identification
     and discernment, 75-76
     and knowledge, 65-66
     and personal concern, 129-130
Immobility, and silence, 120
Imset, 195
Independence, and serenity, 117
Individualization, 191
Ingratitude, 124
Intermediate *Ka. See* Permanent Witness
Intestines, 26, 103, 196
Intuitive state, 200

Jackal, 194-195
Joy, 181-182
     and thankfulness, 122-124
Jupiter, 23

Ka, 7-8, 34, 43, 55, 150, 151, 157, 201-204
Karma, and reincarnation, 143-152
Knowledge, 65-73
     and appropriate gesture, 118
     Master of, 153
     and milieu, 80

Lao-tse, 5, 6, 120
Left side, 21
Life, 183
     fire of, 27-38
Light, 82-83, 158-159
     and joy, 181
Limbs, 21
Liver, 23, 26, 57, 103, 195
     and sex, 92
Liver-bile-brain circuit, 25
Logos, 43

Love
vs. desire and need, 91-94
Master of, 153
vs. sentimentality, 139
Lucifer, 36
Lungs, 20, 26, 102, 195
Lymph, 22-23

Man, 195
consciousness in, 32-37
Master(s), 107-108
of Wisdom, 153-159
Masterhood, and milieu, 80
Means, and milieu, 78
Mediation
of heart, 59-61
and watchfulness, 101-104
Mental state, 200
Mercury, 21
Middle way
and mediation of heart, 59-61
and Way of the Heart, 56-57, 58-59
Milieu, 77-79
and tendencies, 79-83
Myself, and knowledge, 67-68

Nature, and Spirit, 184
Need, vs. desire and love, 91-94
Neter, 49
Nicodemus, 143

Obstacles, 127-128
false pity, 132-135
personal concern, 128-130
quest for sanctity, 135-138
routine, 140
satisfaction, 139-140
sentimentality, 138-139
wrong notion of Providence, 130-132
Old Testament, 64
Orientation, of body, 21-22
Original Fire, 156
Osirian Consciousness, 50
Osirian rhythm, 36
Osiris, 49-50

Pain, 132
Pardon, 12
Peace, 177-179
Pendulum, 95-99
Perfect silence, 120

Permanent Witness, 33-37, 40, 151
and conduct, 105, 108
and duel, 43-49
and knowledge, 66, 69
and mediation, 102-103
and sense of Presence, 114
and Way of the Heart, 55, 56, 57
Personal concern, 128-130
Personal Consciousness, 46, 48, 59
and conduct, 106
Personality, 129
and duel, 43-49
and ka, 151
Personal Self, 47-48
Personal Will, 17
vs. Will to the Light, 39, 40
Pingala, 26, 27
Pity, false, 132-135
Power, of heart, 57-58
Presence, sense of, 113-114
Providence, wrong notion of, 130-132
Psychospiritual states, 199-204
Pyramid Texts, 4

Qebhsenuf, 196
Quantitative mentality, 2
Question, great, 13-14
Rationalist, learned, 3
Reason faculties, and divine truth, 3-4
Red crown, 50
Reincarnation, and karma, 143-152
Remorse, 136
Right side, 21
Routine, 140
Royal principle, 5

Sage, and divine wisdom, 3-4
Salt, 21
Samadhi, 47
Sanctity, quest for, 135-138
Satan, 36
Satisfaction, 139-140
Selection, 191
Self, 46
and human triad, 33-37
Self-knowledge, 15
Sentimentality, 138-139
Serenity, 116-118
Sexual problem, 91-94
Shame, 136
Shushumna, 26, 27

Silence, 119-122
Simplicity, 60
Sin, 12
Skin, 193
Small intestine, 103, 196
Son of Man, and Son of God, 183-185
Soul, 200
  in ancient Egypt, 200-204
Spine, 20-21, 26
Spirit, 130, 200
  fountain and gifts of, 63-64
  and generosity, 125
  and nature, 184
Spiritual Consciousness. *See* Spiritual
  Witness
Spiritual Heart, 34, 43, 59
  and conduct, 106
Spiritual Principle, 157
Spiritual Self, 48, 56
Spiritual Witness, 33-37, 40 59
  and conduct, 105, 106, 108
  and duel, 43-49
  and knowledge, 66
  and sense of Presence, 114
  and serenity, 116
  and Way of the Heart, 55, 57
Spleen, 24, 57
Stomach, 26, 82, 103, 194-195
Substance, generation of, 192
Sulfur, 21
Suppression, 93
Suprahuman realm, keys to, 49-51

Tao, 128, 131
  and appropriate gesture, 119
Tendencies, and milieu, 79-83

Thankfulness, 122-124
Thyroid gland, 21
Transformation, of blood, 191
Transparency, and serenity, 117
Tree of Exchange, 102
Triad, human, 33-37
Truth
  divine, 3-4
  toward one, 4-8

Universal Consciousness, 31-32, 46-47

Vital force, 199
  synthesis and coordination, 23-25
Vital states, of bodily organs, 189-191

Watchfulness, and mediation, 101-104
Way, 39
Way of the Heart, 51, 55-56
  and mediation of heart, 59-61
  and middle way, 56-57
  and power of heart, 57-59
White crown, 50
Willpower, vs. concentration, 115
Will to the Light, 17
  and pendulum, 96
  vs. personal will, 39, 40
Wisdom
  divine, 3-4
  Lao-tse on, 6
  Masters of, 153-159
World of Causes, 20

Yoga, 60

Zacchaeus, 138

A NOTE ON THE WORKS OF
R. A. AND ISHA SCHWALLER DE LUBICZ

Inner Traditions is privileged to present a rare moment in the full understanding of Western civilization. After many years of studying the medieval legacy in religious, Hermetic, and esoteric fields, and their manifestation in the Gothic cathedrals, R.A. and Isha Schwaller de Lubicz experienced a recognition of that same expression in the monuments of the Pharaohs.

Their work represents the first important breakthrough in our comprehension of Egypt since Champollion deciphered the Rosetta Stone. This penetration of the monuments' symbolism and intuitive reading of the glyphs situates Egypt, not Greece, as the cradle of our Western heritage. Often in the style of an oral teaching, the de Lubiczs' work serves as a guide that will initiate the reader into the authentic tone, structure, and mentality of Egyptian wisdom.

Both R. A. and Isha Schwaller de Lubicz were masters of a broad spectrum of knowledge. Familiarity with any discipline will enhance the understanding of their work—philosophy, astronomy, geology, biology, or, for the very perceptive, poetry and art. Yet it is not the de Lubiczs' grasp of the many departments of knowledge alone which is masterful, but their transcendent understanding which qualifies them to question the achievements of our civilization. The work of R. A. and Isha Schwaller de Lubicz offers direction not only to the spiritual seeker, but to the scientist and the philosopher as well.

SACRED SCIENCE
The King of Pharaonic Theocracy
R. A. Schwaller de Lubicz
Illustrated by Lucie Lamy
Translated from the French by A. and G. VandenBroeck
ISBN 0-89281-222-2
$14.95 paperback

The royal principle, in humanity as well as in nature, is capable of transforming the imperfect elements of a type into the perfection of its own nature. This process of transformation is a science, held sacred by the sages, and is the concern of the pharaonic texts cited in these pages.

Schwaller de Lubicz contrasts two poles of mentality, the modern and the ancient Egyptian, or pharaonic. Our rationalistic mentality is oriented toward the acquisition of technological data and its utilitarian application, and under the pretext of facilitating life, the unbridled search for new inventions hones man's egotism and leads him to destruction. Opposed in the extreme, the pharaonic mentality, based on a gnosis (knowledge of causes), shows its *certitude* by the aim and directives it assigns to earthly existence.

"Schwaller's grand synthesis reveals, once and for all, the full extent and significance of the knowledge of Ancient Egypt."
—**Parabola**

THE EGYPTIAN MIRACLE
An Introduction to the Wisdom of the Temple
R. A. Schwaller de Lubicz
Illustrated by Lucie Lamy
Translated from the French by A. and G. VandenBroeck
ISBN 0-89281-008-4
$16.95 paperback

The Egyptian Miracle is an indispensable guide to the transcendental science expressed by the architecture, the texts, and the proportions of the temple. Here, the author evokes an intuitive comprehension—the "intelligence of the heart"—to penetrate the essence of the symbol-object, opening the door to the mystic temple.

Introducing the High Science of Egypt and of Pythagoras, de Lubicz discusses measure and how it relates to man, to the esoteric significance of number, and to the geometric elements. He also offers remarkable insights into the physics of alchemy, the nature of color and sound, and the esoteric structure of the planetary system, concluding with essential philosophical texts and initiatic teachings from his untranslated masterwork, *Le Temple de l'Homme*. He encourages students to orient themselves in the mentality required for penetrating the science of the sages.

"As a contemporary renaissance man, R. A. Schwaller de Lubicz, who in his youth studied painting with Matisse, may fall into that category of genius shared by such luminaries as Rudolf Steiner and Emanuel Swedenborg. He combined the talents of social reformer, artist, scientist, visionary, and mystic to formulate ideas that were so far ahead of their time they seemed doomed, until recently, to be ignored."
—EastWest

THE TEMPLE IN MAN
Sacred Architecture and the Perfect Man
R. A. Schwaller de Lubicz
ISBN 0-89281-021-1
$10.95 paperback

Following fifteen years of on-site research at Luxor Temple in Egypt, including careful measurement of every block and inscription, the author reveals how each detail of masonry and symbolic art expreses an element of the Egyptians' comprehensive knowledge of man's physical and spiritual anatomy. He shows how the plan of the temple was rigorously based on human proportions and was actually designed to represent Pharaoh, symbolic of the Perfect Man, the final stage of man's evolution toward the Divine.

SYMBOL AND THE SYMBOLIC
Ancient Egypt, Science, and the
Evolution of Consciousness
R. A. Schwaller de Lubicz
ISBN 0-89281-022-X
$8.95 paperback

Discover why true progress in human thought must incorporate the "symbolizing" faculty of intelligence, developed and refined in the Temple Culture of ancient Egypt, and reflected in the hieroglyphs that have come down to us undisturbed. De Lubicz contrasts the mechanistic, analytic mentality of modern science with the synthetic, vitalist mentality of ancient Egyptian Sacred Science, showing that only a symbolic mentality can think without objectifying, enabling us to overcome the inherent limitations of reason.

NATURE WORD
Verbe Nature
R. A. Schwaller de Lubicz
ISBN 0-89281-036-X
$10.95 paperback

In this remarkable and enigmatic work, composed immediately upon his return from Egypt in 1952, the noted French esotericist R. A. Schwaller de Lubicz conveys to modern consciousness insights derived from a lifetime of experience and study in the ancient and sacred traditions of humanity. His theme is "the intelligence of the heart," our innate, functional way of thinking, which is in harmony with nature and enables us to understand life and living things.

A STUDY OF NUMBERS
A Guide to the Constant Creation of the Universe
R. A. Schwaller de Lubicz
ISBN 0-89281-112-9
$9.95 paperback

In this, his first work, published originally in 1917, R. A. Schwaller de Lubicz presents an absorbing account of the living, universal, qualitative, and casual reality of numbers, based on the idea of Unity. Starting from the irreducible one, he shows the unfolding of creation through the cycles of polarization, ideation, and formation, with topics that include numbers, values, and relations; the disengagement of numbers; the harmonic basis of numbers; the development of values; and the establishment of harmony.

ESOTERISM AND SYMBOL
R. A. Schwaller de Lubicz
ISBN 0-89281-014-9
$8.95 paperback

Esoterism and Symbol initiates the reader into the tone, structure, and mentality of ancient Egyptian knowledge, the wellspring of all Western theology and science. It is a redefinition of those concepts that are basic to the pharaonic transmission.

Making a distinction between two kinds of human intelligence, Schwaller de Lubicz shows that symbols are conventional representations of cerebral intelligence, derived from the recording of observed facts; while the hieroglyph is a non-conventional form of communication with the unique ability speak directly to the innate "intelligence of the heart."

All esoteric, spiritual teaching is addressed to this intelligence. It can be neither written nor spoken, and has nothing in common with deliberate concealment of truth. The preparation needed to grasp it is not a matter of learned knowledge but of intuitive capacity, allowing humanity to move toward self-knowledge and the Divine.

Esoterism and Symbol explores the "process of becoming" as it relates to consciousness and is revealed in all of nature; the relationship of "apparent life" and the life behind appearances; the kinship between humanity and the mineral, plant, and animal kingdoms; the mystery of the formation of substance into matter; myth, Kabbalah, and the stages of awareness leading to "Cosmic Consciousness."

HER-BAK
The Living Face of Ancient Egypt
Isha Schwaller de Lubicz
$12.95 paperback

This vivid re-creation of the spiritual life of ancient Egypt is seen through the eyes of young Her-Bak, candidate for initiation into the sublime mysteries of the Temple. This fictional account traces his development through the stages of his spiritual ascent, from the lessons Nature teaches him as a young boy, his education as a scribe, and finally as a candidate for service in the Temple. Isha Schwaller de Lubicz based her account on years of research at the temples of Luxor and Karnak.

HER-BAK
Egyptian Initiate
Isha Schwaller de Lubicz
ISBN 0-89281-002-5
$14.95 paperback

This second and independent volume continues Her-Bak's spiritual quest, as he is initiated into the Inner Temple and follows his progressive penetration of the esoteric aspects of the Egyptian Mystery teachings, showing the evolution of one individual's life through the phases of temple training. The Her-Bak stories are set between the Twentieth and Twenty-first Dynasties, at Karnak in the Valley of the Kings.

JOURNEY INTO THE LIGHT
The Three Principles of Man's Awakening
Isha Schwaller de Lubicz
ISBN 0-89281-038-6
$14.95 paperback

A companion volume to the author's *Opening of the Way,* this text, in the form of a novel, portrays the transformative encounter of the modern, scientific, and rational mentality with the suprarational, spiritual intelligence that guides us on the Path of the Mysteries. With scholarship and deep insight the author traces the root of knowledge through Buddhism, Hinduism, and Christianity all the way back to the sacred science of Egypt. In so doing she enables us to discover the symbolism and rites that are the bridge to the spiritual life.

The 20th century setting of the novel offers us practical advice on incorporating ancient wisdom into contemporary life and challenges us to realize, in the midst of this conditioned and confused world, our "conscious presence" so that we may free ourselves and transform the world around us.

These and other Inner Traditions titles are available at many fine bookstores or, to order directly from the publisher, send a check or money order for the total amount, payable to Inner Traditions, plus $3.00 shipping and handling for the first book and $1.00 for each additional book to:

Inner Traditions
P.O. Box 956
Rochester, VT   05767

Be sure to request a free catalog.